# Daughter of the Sea

*My Voyage to Freedom and Womanhood*

## Hiep Thi Le

Jill Powell
jillp@daughterofthesea.net
www.daughterofthesea.net

# Daughter of the Sea

Copyright © 2021 by Heip Thi Le & Jill Powell

All rights reserved. No part of this book may be reproduced or transmitted in any form or by any means, electronic or mechanical, including photocopying, recording, or by any information storage and retrieval system, without written permission of the publisher.

MAPLE LEAF PUBLISHING INC.
3rd Floor 4915 54 St Red Deer,
Alberta T4N 2G7 Canada
General Inquiries & Customer Service
Phone: 1-(403)-356-0255
Toll Free: 1-(888)-498-9380
Email: info@mapleleafpublishinginc.com

Because of the dynamic nature of the Internet, any web addresses or links contained in this book may have changed since publication and may no longer be valid. The views expressed in the work are solely those of the author and do not necessarily reflect the views of the publisher, and the publisher hereby disclaims any responsibility for them.

ISBN

Paperback: 978-1-77419-081-4

Hardback: 978-1-77419-123-1

eBook: 978-1-77419-082-1

## Contents

Headwaters . . . . . . . . . . . . . . . . . . 4
Outgoing Tide . . . . . . . . . . . . . . . . . 7
Calm Before the Storm . . . . . . . . . . . .14
Rough Water . . . . . . . . . . . . . . . . . .19
Sucker Hole . . . . . . . . . . . . . . . . . . 25
Life Ring . . . . . . . . . . . . . . . . . . . . 29
Victoria Harbor . . . . . . . . . . . . . . . . 34
Queen Rat . . . . . . . . . . . . . . . . . . .51
Land of Diamonds . . . . . . . . . . . . . . 56
Death of a King . . . . . . . . . . . . . . . . 67
Sea Sisters . . . . . . . . . . . . . . . . . . 72
Sea Birds . . . . . . . . . . . . . . . . . . . 79
Crow's Nest . . . . . . . . . . . . . . . . . .91
Landlocked . . . . . . . . . . . . . . . . . . 97
I'll Wind . . . . . . . . . . . . . . . . . . . . 105
Safe Harbor . . . . . . . . . . . . . . . . . . 111
Smooth Sailing . . . . . . . . . . . . . . . . 122

# Acknowledge

I am so grateful to Hiep for the time She allowed me to share in her life. I think of her often and reflect back our painful conversations as well as the laughter of her funny stories.

I want to dedicate this book to Hiep to helping her dream come true and teaching me inspiration, perseverance, patience, knowledge and appreciation for life.

I always want to thank my chosen family, my friends, my best friend, Lori, and the people along the way that kept me inspired to continue to make Hiep's dream come true.

I also extend a very special thanks to my Developmental Writer, Mr. Jay Wurts, who has extended his help to me on more than one occasion to help this book come to fruition. Without his patience, care and mentoring, Hiep's memoirs manuscript would not have the essence of innocence that She so desired. I am very grateful and humble for his assistance.

Hiep and I became friends as we discussed that her story and adventure from Vietman should be shared with the world.

As I, a mother of Vietnamese boy, Noah Tuyen, could not locate such resources about their culture, religion, food or the struggles they endured so he could acknowledge and love the people that came before him.

Gabriel, my second son, who sounded like Hiep at times, would often whisper keep on dreaming. I love them both more than they will ever know. Dreams can true with dedication, positive energy and faith in your path.

-Jill Powell

# 1

## *Headwaters*

My life began over the water because that's where everyone lived. When you depend on fish for a living, it pays to keep an eye on them.

Our stilt-huts stood like storky bird on the restless shore of the Song Hang River. Truthfully, with their thatched roofs and tangled poles they didn't look much different from the rippling paddies and bamboo thickets that surrounded the strip of dirt which served as our main road. Before my fifth birthday, I was taught the song about my village called An Hai. But who cared? I never left it, so I never had to ask strangers how to get back. Adults back then cared about a lot of things that didn't make sense.

Across the wide Song Hang (which changed color daily: sometimes silver blue; sometimes muddy brown; other times clear as rainwater, even when the shore was clogged with branches and dead insects) lay the city of Da Nang, just on the edge of seeing. I don't know how it got that name but somehow it seemed to fit. I never saw people there—too far away from even the best vantage on our slippery roof—and its residents never came to visit, so I thought it might be a mirage or a trick played by Father Dragon, who lived in the sky above our house, or a joke by Mother Fairy—the two Spirits from whom all Vietnamese are descended. They were our Adam and Eve and each of us inherited some of their magical powers, which were reflected in the world around us. For that blessing we might thank Mother Fairy's heavenly prodigy, Quang Am, the Goddess of Mercy, who taught us there was a time and place for everything, causes and consequence, and that life was a great unfolding. We depended on the lullabies from Father Dragon and Mother Fairy to teach us the facts and rituals of life because our parents were too busy or shy to talk about them. Dutifully, kids and parents remembered these High Spirits in our prayers and cradle songs, especially Mama, for whom singing was just another way to breathe.

Our other guides through life were dead. No, really. Mama and Father left food and cups of liquor for them on our family altar and burned incense to get their attention. These spirits needed food to keep up their strength so they could protect the living and help us use the gifts we'd received from our Creators. I never saw these dead ancestors myself, but the food always disappeared so there must've been something to it. One time, I caught my younger sister Dimples drinking a splash of brandy left for my long-departed grandmother so after I told on her to Mama, Father warned her that tampering with our altar-food would provoke ghosts to haunt her forever. That scared her off, so even when we went hungry (which seemed more often than not, depending on how close the soldiers from North or South rummaged around An Hai) our ancestors never did. I never saw these fighters either, but I knew when they were there because of the terrifying noises they made at night.

Okay, you're wondering that if I didn't see them, how did I know they made the booms and tat-a-tats that silenced the frogs and crickets? I learned about them mostly by eavesdropping on our neighbors after we'd spent a night in our family bunker. I hated that muddy, moldy old hole that was shaped just like a grave. We couldn't light candles or cook food and when we peed or pooed we dug a hole where we squatted then covered it up like a cat. I learned from these neighbors that cousin Nhanh had been a soldier for the South and that Father was descended from a long line of Kung-Fu fishermen. He'd studied herbal medicine with the Buddhist monks at Marble Mountain and became our village healer. Because he had access to every house and knew just about everyone's secrets, he served the South a part-time spy when he made his rounds, keeping track of who was where. He muttered chants while mixing betel ointment and spat holy liquor onto wounds and broken bones to make them better. You'd think with all that talent he could cure the lice we kids carried around like hitchhikers on our head, picking them off and eating them as snacks, but he never did. The bugs liked me best, so Mama shaved my head and swatted my hands when I scratched the sores. With my big bald head, crooked neck, and malnourished pot belly, I looked like a bug myself and was the butt of everyone's jokes. Lacking playmates never bothered me, because I found an invisible friend in Mister Dragon who never belittled me or argued back. I whispered to him for hours, felt his Dragon breath on my cheeks when I stood in the river breeze and heard his silver laugh in the rippling waves. Sometimes I got so involved that I missed Mama's call to dinner or Father's commands to finish a chore. I guess they thought I was a little loopy, but they only heard half of the conversation.

Gradually, fighting stopped in the forest and paddies around An Hai. A year passed, then another and another but villagers continued to vanish: one by one, in pairs, even whole families. Those remaining met each disappearance with silence then whispers which turned to gossip. I started listening and got an earful. One uncle who had been in the North left the village as soon as he returned because, as one neighbor said, "He held dangerous opinions." Dangerous to who? I didn't get it. Eventually, cousin Nhanh disappeared, too, along with some village women who were known to complain about everything. Neighbors said they all had to be re-educated by men who wore yellow stars on their hats. This interested me greatly since the only things I'd been taught in An Hai were how to tote water from our well and pull fish baskets up the riverbank. Beyond the sighs of Father Dragon and chirping birds who spoke for Mother Fairy, my knowledge of the world was sorely lacking. I, too, wondered where everyone went, but I'd also learned from my parents not to ask too many questions.

So along with prayers and lullabies, gossip became my teacher and our village continued to shrink. People said they had no idea where their relatives went, or why. Only one old woman, one day, let the answer slip. "The departed now live under the White Dragon," she said, so close to her ancestors that she no longer cared who listened. "That dragon's name is America."

# 2

## *Outgoing Tide*

My older brother Tiny and younger brother Brat, along with my older sister Pudgy and younger sister Dimples (yes, I was always in the middle), awoke at midnight in our usual dogpile on the platform bed we shared.

"What's that?" Dimples reacted to the loud bang.

"Tet!" Tiny sat up. "The first firecracker of 1979! Happy New Year!"

"Get your big monster-diseased head off me, Twiggy!" Pudgy, a heavy sleeper whom anyone awoke at their own risk, pushed me away with her elbow. I rubbed my eyes and didn't take it personally. I was short and except for a wormy potbelly, skinny for my age. With my head still shaved to heal lice-sores and a neck curved from carrying it around, I looked like a melon on a crooked stick. I thought about telling Pudgy that I was sorry for polluting her arm, but she didn't apologize for pushing me through the mosquito net onto the floor, so we called it even. Tet, the lunar New Year and Vietnam's biggest holiday always started with a bang. This time it was a midnight firecracker followed by me hitting the floor.

By the time we gathered on our porch, the night air was alive with neighbors laughing and setting-off fireworks, though nobody left their homes. After all, if ancestral spirits were to bless us, they had to know where we were. Mama now appeared behind us holding Fly Swat, our new baby brother. He was wailing, as usual, but nobody heard him in all the racket. Mama's face glowed like ours.

The nice thing about Tet—besides providing an excuse to make noise—is that everybody gets more of the two things that mattered most in An Hai: life and money. Only city people track days on a calendar, and since we villagers just notice Buddhist holidays and the dates related to planting rice and running fish, Tet serves as everyone's birthday—that way it's easy to remember. So that midnight, when the first firecracker went off, I got promoted to eight just as Fly Swat got promoted to two, even though he was only born last month. Even better, on the second day of Tet we kids got li-si from our relatives—red envelopes filled with cash—and new clothes, when our parents or relatives could afford them. My two sisters got nice dresses from our aunts, who seemed to think I was a boy (maybe because of my bald head), so Mama made me flowered pajamas from my yard of government-rationed fabric. I actually loved those PJ's more than Pudgy and Dimples liked their factory dresses. After all, Mama had personally made them for me. It was nice to feel special about something other than having a big head covered with sores.

So Tet turned everyone into kids. Even Father, who was often grumpy, got caught-up in the holiday spirit and smiled, showing his four brass teeth that glinted in the fireworks like gold. He'd lost them as a teenager and been given implants. Like all Vietnamese, he was known to other adults by his family number-name, which was Seven. That meant he was sixth born because the father is always Number One. Similarly, Father's older brother, my Uncle Six, was fifth-born but he was sometimes called "Six Fingers" because of a digit lost in his youth. Father had an acquired nickname, too. Because of his shiny front teeth, adults called him Seven Fire. This ornament, though, did not make him sparkle. Like most other Vietnamese fathers, he was very distant to his kids. Like dogs who love their owner despite mistreatment, we basked in his rare attention even when it was bad: like harsh words for failure or a parental swat when we misbehaved. We got good at reading his moods and avoided anything that annoyed him. Tonight on the Eve of Tet, though, his smile was expansive and our small crimes blew past him like smoke from the fireworks. Soon, the pops and bangs began to fizzle and our village gave the night back to the crickets.

Thirteen-year old Tiny was more like Father. "The last firecracker is the best," he said in his breaking voice. "It's just like me. Cool and patient, taking its time before it blows. BANG!" He laughed maniacally but it made me think that Tiny, like Father, could probably handle anything. Because our government food ration was always small—one bowl of pig bran with dried potatoes or wheat flour for each person every day—he was especially good at pinching vegetables from other gardens, but only for us kids. Father would punch the daylights out of Tiny if he caught Tiny dishonoring our family name; and if Father didn't catch him, Mama would do the honors. Stealing is always a crime, even when done by an empty stomach.

Anyway, as the activity in neighbors' yards died down, Mama called our attention back to our house. No matter what people said about her, Mama was still the prettiest lady in the village: with rosy fair skin, slim legs and flat tummy, and hair in a tight black bun suggesting an orderly mind. And she was fertile. That meant a lot to our gossipy neighbors: seven births with six children still living. If anyone had bothered to teach her to read and write, she could have written the book on Vietnamese motherhood.

With baby Fly Swat stuck to her hip like a barnacle, she called us for Father's annual blessing—another Tet ritual. We lined up on our porch by age and Father asked our ancestors (now invisibly in attendance) to bless and protect us for another year, especially when we ventured out on the treacherous South China Sea. That made sense for him because he was a deep-sea fisherman, although it was the first time he even hinted that a family member might go too—that just didn't happen unless you were an uncle or teenaged son big enough to do a man's work. Even to a dumb little twerp like me something, well, smelled fishy.

Father distributed sweet bean pudding to each of us in descending order of age, saying it was to remind us of the sweetness of Tet and a foretaste of the bountiful year he hoped we would all enjoy. Before giving each kid a bowl, though, he addressed us by our family nickname and recalled a little something from our past. Family nicknames were just about all we kids possessed. They evoked something about us that was distinctive and spared us the risk of using our given name which, if said aloud, might summon a wandering ghost to inhabit our body, mistaking it for his. Most people never heard their formal name until they were older than us, so that was probably a wise precaution.

"Tiny," Father said, clearing his throat like a high official or a doctor pronouncing his diagnosis, "you were no bigger than my fist when you crawled from your mother's womb." That was too much information, and it certainly didn't apply to Tiny now.

Pudgy, our bossy oldest sister, was next. Come on, Father—make it good!

"Pudgy," he said, "you came into this world as round as a watermelon," a condition she never got over, munching incessantly on lice the way a rich kid might eat candy. I laughed and Pudgy jabbed me with her elbow.

"Twiggy," Uh oh, my turn, "you fell into life with a plop, a tiny bundle of sticks and bones." Fair enough. Is this the year you do something about my head sores? I accepted my bowl of red pudding with a humble bow.

"Dimples," he moved on to his youngest daughter, two years junior to me, "as soon as you showed your face, your smile lit up the room!" As a matter of fact, it still did. I loved my dear little sister, despite my loathing for the cute little dip in her right cheek that magically appeared when she smiled. Where Pudgy was all boss-and-bluster, our surrogate mother when Mama was gone, Dimples was clever with a talent for getting her way. She was also smart enough to act stupid when that was the thing to do. That wasn't necessary for me. My ignorance came naturally.

We ate our sweet pudding with respectful restraint and when we finally went to bed, I dreamed about the Water Princess Father once said he'd show me if I ever grew big enough to sail on his boat. That would be the day!

The next day, guests with Li-si envelopes were supposed to arrive, so I sat in my favorite waiting place (the steps by our house that led up from the river) and overheard our neighbors talking about something that happened during the night.

"They left before the morning wind came up," one lady said, "while the stars were still in the east."

"Who?" the other asked. "Both of them?"

"Three of them. Seven Fire and his older brother, Six Fingers, plus Tiny, the oldest son. Gone. Poof! Just like that!"

"It had to be planned—"

"Of course it was planned. Nobody works on Tet, not even the shore patrol. Who wants to start-off the coming year with hard labor? Everyone sleeps like a log. You can do anything you want."

"Bastards!" the other lady said. "Sneaky traitors! When they're caught they'll go away for a good long time. And anyone who talks to their stinking family should get sent away, too. Look! There's one of the daughters, Twiggy, over there on the steps—just sitting there staring at us!"

They gave me the evil eye and gathered up the beans they'd been shucking and scuttled away like two crabs. I bounded up the steps into our house.

"Mama! Mama?" She was not in the house so I went to the back yard where she was bathing Fly Swat by the well. "Mama—you won't believe what I heard!" Tears rolled down her pretty face.

"Mama, what's wrong?" Now I was worried. Mama always said it was bad luck to cry on Tet, or even to think unhappy thoughts. This problem must be a lulu. Pudgy, Dimples, and Brat were standing nearby—just standing: not doing chores, not playing, not doing anything. Just staring at Mama. They were white-faced, like me.

"Where's Tiny?" Now I was scared.

"He's out," she wiped her cheek, sniffed, then let out a short breath before continuing. "He's on an errand."

"Where's Father?"

"He's—out, too."

"Mama," I continued, words tumbling out, "the two ladies next door said Uncle Six and Father were traitors and—"

The flat of her hand stung my cheek. Mama had never hit me before. That alone would've started me crying except it was bad luck.

Mama carried Fly Swat into the house and we followed, quiet as mice. Usually, the second day of Tet saw at least a few relatives and old friends drop by with Li-si or a little candy or with some left-overs from the first night's banquet, but this Tet the house stayed quiet all day—not a single caller until an old soldier, one of Father's friends, came and met with Mama by our front gate. We kids had gone to bed, but despite Pudgy's snoring, I was still awake and heard their solemn conversation.

"What went wrong?" the old soldier asked.

"I found the rowboat man at dawn," Mama answered, followed by a short, frustrated breath. "My husband thought we'd all been caught so he and Tiny went on without us. The rowboat man said they got aboard the launch okay but the captain saw patrol boat lights in Da Nang and sailed away without waiting for anyone else."

"You left my name out of it, right?" the old soldier looked like he'd seen his own ghost.

"Oh, sure," Mama said. "Nobody knows you had anything to do with it—although you're taking a big risk coming here. Half the village knows about them by now."

The old soldier didn't wait for more news, but disappeared into the darkness, lickety-split. Fly Swat started crying so I pretended to wake up as Mama came to get him and shush us big kids back to sleep. It took a while, but her lullaby from the other room finally put me under. That night, I did not dream of sea princesses or Father Dragon or Mother Fairy, but black water and stormy skies.

The next morning as we kids ate breakfast, Mama met two policemen at our front door. One peeked around her shoulder to the inside of the house. When it was obvious they weren't leaving, Mama stepped onto the porch, Fly Swat on her hip, drawing their attention away from us. We continued to eat, bug-eyed in silence, until Dimples asked, "What's going on?"

"Shut up, you little dummy!" Pudgy was in command while Mama was busy, so we all did what she said. When Pudgy was sure the cops weren't coming in, she leaned over to us and whispered, "Father and Tiny are gone. They ran away and left us. Now the police are going to take Mama."

"No way!" Dimples said. Her normally sunny face started to cloud up. Brat, only three, was too busy with his hot yam to know or care what was happening. Pudgy tried to look more pissed than scared, but I could see she, too, was on the verge of tears.

"I know what's going on," I lied because it seemed like the thing to do. I casually picked at the bottom of my bowl. "I heard the neighbor ladies talk yesterday, and Mama talked to one of Father's friends last night. Everything's under control. Everything's okay. After all, it's Tet."

# 3

## *Calm Before the Storm*

Unfortunately, my well-intended lie didn't change the facts. The policemen stayed on our porch for an hour then left with Mama and Fly Swat. Mama only had time to stick her head inside and tell us she was going to a police station on the edge of town and would "be right back." That didn't happen either.

We kids finished breakfast, did the dishes then tried to remember what we were supposed to do when adults weren't around. I got water from the well. Pudgy washed some clothes—just her own—and pounded them too long and too hard before hanging them up to dry. Dimples just moped and Brat continued being useless. Finally the sun dropped and we all got hungry so Pudgy fed us some boiled yams, setting aside a covered bowl to take to Mama.

"Put these little dorks to bed if I don't get home by dark," she told me like a soldier-sergeant. I saw no reason to argue. Unfortunately, though the sun was down and village lamps came on, Pudgy returned with Mama's bowl still full.

"What happened?" I asked. "Couldn't you find the police house?"

"I found it," Pudgy answered. "But Mama told me to pretend to eat the food in front of her and never come back. She said that if the guards knew us kids could look after ourselves, they'd never let her out."

"So what do we do?" I asked.

"Well, you can shut up and go to bed. That goes for the rest of you, too."

"What about the aunties who gave you and Dimples those nice dresses?" I said. "Won't they take care of us if they know Mama and Father are gone?"

"Don't count on it. Mama said everybody's afraid to come near our house. That's why she told the police that if they keep her, us kids will starve. She said to sit tight and not talk to anyone, so that's what we'll do. Any questions?" Pudgy made a big fist. Discussion over.

Two days later, Mama came home. We gang-hugged her at the door and pulled her inside. She looked tired but happy to see us. Fly Swat looked healthy and just as out-of-it as ever. He sucked his fingers and made big eyes at the thatched ceiling but didn't make a peep.

Mama inspected each of us for bumps and bruises and other signs of accidents or misfortune, of which there were none except for my lice scabs and dark circles under all our eyes. At least Pudgy had kept us fed.

"Okay, so here's what we have to do," Mama said after unplugging Fly Swat from his liquid lunch. "We're all under house arrest. Does everyone know what that means?"

Obviously, Dimples didn't and if Brat understood he would forget it in a minute.

"It means we all have to stay indoors," I said, showing how well-qualified I was to run things in case anything happened to Pudgy.

"Right. We can go outdoors to get water and tend our garden and do laundry and whatnot, but we can't leave our yard and for sure we can't go near the river. The policemen said two aunties can bring us our daily food ration, but only when a policeman comes with them and only if they don't stay to visit. That goes for the neighbor kids, too."

Actually, things could've been worse. Although we were shut-ins, Mama was a good storyteller and each night told us the further adventures of Lady Kieu, a legendary heroine from our country's past. Lady Kieu, too, once lived under a different Dragon—perhaps in the same mysterious place that had already lured so many villagers.

"Where is the White Dragon?" I asked in the middle of one story, confirming Pudgy's suspicion that I was stupid.

"A long way away," Mama answered.

"They say that's where cousin Nhanh lives. Are Father and Tiny living there, too? When will they come home?"

Mama smiled her pretty smile, let out a short breath and simply said, "Lady Kieu always comes home at the end of her adventures—didn't I tell you that?"

I knew what she meant: That she didn't want to talk about Father and Tiny or cousin Nhanh or anything that had to do with the White Dragon—code-word for "America," as I would soon find out—and just mentioning it meant you could be hauled-in by the police or questioned by nosey neighbors, even if you were a kid. In our case, ignorance was not just bliss, it was life.

On the other hand, information goes two ways. I decided that if I kept my mouth shut and my ears open, I could sit on my favorite steps and learn a thing or two from our neighbors. In fact, the two crab ladies got so used to seeing me there that they ignored me altogether as they went about their chores.

"People are leaving the country left and right," one said, wrestling with a particularly tough tuber. "It's amazing there's anyone left to do the work!"

"Except for soldiers and policemen!" the other said. "We always have plenty of those."

"Well, laugh all you want, but good citizens like us have to keep an eye on things. The block chairmen and police can't be everywhere."

That was true, and it worked in Mama's favor. After a week or two of good behavior, the local magistrate called off his watchdogs and Mama was allowed to go to market again—not just to shop, but to sell the home-made shrimp paste for which she was a village legend.

Still, the air in our neighborhood was tense. Neighbors nodded as we passed but seldom spoke. People who'd constantly asked Mama to exchange her shrimp paste for a favor now found they could do without it. Kids ran when my sisters and I approached so our only playmates were each other, which got old very fast. Fly Swat was a good listener but didn't have much to say, so I started hanging out with Mama, but even she started behaving oddly.

For example, she almost always came home late now from An Hai market and would sometimes slip away at night after we'd been put to bed. Sometimes she'd leave on one errand as soon as she'd returned from another—very strange for the attentive, disciplined woman I knew. Pudgy had been our family cook since she turned eight, with Mama contributing the occasional, special meal, but since our release from house arrest she'd become a stranger to our kitchen. One rainy afternoon at the start of the summer monsoon, she was especially late from the market. She shook out her rain hat and left her muddy sandals on the porch, and since the other kids were busy elsewhere, I chose that moment to confront her.

"Mama, why are you always away?"

"Hmph," she snorted like a bull. "How many jobs do you think it takes to keep this family going? Now be a good girl and go find your little brother. I don't like him playing outside in this bad weather."

I did as I was told, and it was a good thing, too. The wind and rain got worse and at sunset Mama moved us into the worship room with its concrete floor—the place we kept our Buddhist shrine. Father Dragon really tore up the sky that night—with his fire-breath and great gusts from his nostrils and invisible talons that tore up whole trees. When we peered out after a noisy, sleepless night, most of the house was gone.

"Okay, you kids clean this up," Mama said, finding her hat but leaving her basket. "I have to go to work. Stack what we can use by the steps. I'll go through it when I get home. We'll sleep in the worship room until I get the roof back on."

Then she left, without even saying goodbye. Pudgy went to what was left of our kitchen to scrounge breakfast. "I hope she's not leaving us, too," she mumbled.

"What do you mean?" I asked.

"You're so dumb!" Her gruff tone now had Brat and Dimples crying. I tried to comfort them. Pudgy threw up her hands. "Oh, what's the point? Bawl your stupid heads off! That's what you do best, isn't it? What I meant was I hope Mama doesn't run off like Father and Tiny. Why do you think the police arrested her? Why do you think the neighbors avoid our house? You guys are such idiots!"

This was not news, of course—at least not to me. The crab ladies next door had been hinting about it and I had been thinking of it for weeks but was afraid to say it out loud. Now Pudgy had finally plopped the dead fish on the table. I was kind-of relieved that she did. If we kids were going to have to get-by on our own, we'd better start getting good at it.

But the weeks wore on, big storms came and went, and gradually our house got rebuilt. And Mama stuck with us—or at least the shadow of the woman we used to call mother. Perhaps she was trying to make amends when one evening she brought home some fresh, steaming corn from the market.

"See?" she said, beaming as she unwrapped the goods. "I made lots of money today. We don't have to live like cockroaches, nibbling crumbs from the floor. Here—take a cob. Eat it while it's hot!"

We gathered around and gobbled our corn like pigs. That night, with my first really full tummy since Tet, I went to bed and fell asleep first.

# 4

## *Rough Water*

My good night's sleep was short. Mama woke us just after midnight. She gave us each a set of thick, long-sleeved underclothes and told us to put them on—right now!—then dress in our regular clothes.

"Turn on a lamp," Dimples said in a sleepy voice. "I can't find my shirt." But the fire shooting from Mama's eyes was all the light we needed. A few minutes later we were standing in front of our house, the dusty street soaked in starlight.

"Twiggy, you come with me," she said after ensuring the coast was clear. "The rest of you stay here and wait your turn."

She led me to the muddy shore where a short bridge connected our neighborhood stilt-houses to a dock that served the fishermen. It was a calm, April night. All the boats were out working, many with small lanterns on long poles stretching out to lure the fish. Only one boat was tied to the pier, its bow adorned with Number 6, painted in lucky red letters. As we approached over the squeaky planks, a figure stirred from the shadows on deck. I recognized him as one of An Hai's more respected "fish uncles"—a rough-hewn man in the mold of Father's soldier-friend: steady and trustworthy. We knew him only as "Captain" or "Captain Six" because of the number on his boat. Neighbors said he'd been excused from war duty because his wife was a leper, which explained why she never left their house. Whether that exception was granted so he could stay and take care of her or because other draftees would shun him was not explained, but it didn't matter. Whatever Mama had planned for that night, I knew I was in safe hands.

"You said you'd come earlier," the Captain told Mama in a quiet voice.

"You said you were too sick to go to sea today," she replied.

The captain smiled. "Everybody talks from both sides of their mouth these days. Just the one girl then?"

"No. I'll bring more."

"I may have to push off if the shore patrol comes around," he held out his hand to help me aboard.

"No," Mama pulled me back. "It's everyone or nobody." She glanced around the pier and spotted a small, overturned reed-raft the fisherwomen used to harvest snails, clams, and pincher-fish from the shallows. She pulled up an edge and stuffed me underneath.

"You wait here until I come back," she whispered. "And don't make noise!"

I listened to her bare feet pad off and wondered how long "coming back" would take. Aside from the usual stink of river mud and fish-guts, the small raft reeked of the new wax fisherfolk applied periodically to help keep water out. At first it just made me nauseous, then dizzy. The darkness itself felt heavy—suffocating!—and I thought immediately of the river ghosts who used nights like this to hunt fresh bodies to inhabit.

After forever, I heard the pier-planks creak again. I knew I was supposed to wait, but I could feel the spirits press against me so I pushed my fingers under the rim, ready to help Mama raise it and get on with our adventure, but the footsteps were too heavy for Mama's so I pulled my fingers back and listened.

Phssssttt—somebody struck a match: the acrid smoke of a cigarette. The heavy footsteps resumed then stopped between my raft and the edge of the dock. A man's voice sighed and a stream of water hit the shallows. Pee. Gradually the stream diminished. The man coughed and continued toward the boat.

More minutes. More footsteps. I thought I heard men talking—a policeman hassling the Captain?—but the next voice was my mother's. Risking a pinched ear, I lifted the edge of the raft and crawled out.

"Ma—" Mama's hand clamped over my mouth. She lifted me over the gunwales and into the Captain's hands and onto the deck. "Twiggy, be quiet! Not a peep!" Mama whispered urgently. "Do just what the Captain says."

With that she disappeared. The Captain led me to the stinky cargo hold, partially filled with baskets of fish. It was illuminated by a single oil lamp. He pulled up a splintery floor hatch—a "smuggler's hole," the fishermen called it—and told me to climb in. Thank God the lamp went, too. In the crowded space three faces peered back at me—one of them was Dimples. I had no idea how she boarded ahead of me, but there she was—along with the Captain's eldest son, Hung, a few years older than Tiny. I knew Hung only slightly and everyone considered him a thug: a rough kid, quick to anger. The last face was a stranger—maybe a man from another village. The hatch banged shut and we all leaned toward the lamp.

"Dimples—" I started to say but she put a forefinger to her lips and said, "Shhhh—we're all playing hide-and-seek!"

I heard the captain start the engine—two, three, five false starts before it caught, turning Hung's and the stranger's worried looks into big grins. The tired fishing boat shook and seawater seeped through its ill-fitting planks. We felt the boat lurch and roll as the captain pushed off and pointed the bow downriver.

Hung and the strange man began to talk. The stranger had a queer accent and said Hue several times, so I assumed that's where he was from. He also said America once or twice, so it was pretty clear where we were going—although I had no idea if we would make the entire journey in this little boat or confined to our little space. I had plenty of other questions, too, such as Where are Mama, Pudgy, Brat, and Fly Swat? But before I could raise this important topic, the Captain poked his head into our compartment and said, "Hush up! We're coming to a checkpoint!" then closed the hatch. The stranger turned down the lamp and the last thing I saw in its fading light was Hung's fish knife move up toward Dimple's neck while his other hand covered her mouth. Dimples squeaked like a mouse and I grabbed her hands for comfort, which worked—she shut up—though I was sure Hung would've used that knife on me if the situation required it. The stranger's voice calmed us in the dark. "Okay now," he said in his queer Hue accent, "everybody stay cool, everybody stay quiet. I've got plenty of money. If they discover us, we'll just buy our way out."

I guess that was a comforting thought.

Suddenly the motor stopped. The hull quit vibrating and we lurched to the side like a big fish hooked by the gills. "Pull closer!" a distant voice cried. The boat rocked as new feet clunked to the deck. More unfriendly voices. "An Hai," the Captain said.

"Starting out a little late tonight, aren't you?" the new voice asked.

"Felt a little sick after supper," the Captain answered. "Feeling better, now. Want to take a look below?"

Feet walked over our hatch. Dimples squeaked again but just sounded like one of the boards. The captain lit a new lamp in the fish bay and rays of light slashed through the planks. I saw the Hue man pull his hand from his pocket. It held no money, just a small pistol.

"Hey, get the lead out!" a different voice called from the top deck. More clumping feet and the boat rocked again. After a few muffled words, the engine started—one try, then two, then the most beautiful sound in the world!

After a few minutes, the Captain raised the hatch and said, "All clear, but stay on your toes," then shut the hatch again. We all relaxed. Hung re-lit the lamp and I saw his knife was already sheathed and the Hue man's gun was back in his pocket. Their faces were soaked with sweat and only then did it sink-in how close to death Dimples and I had come—if not from the river policemen, then the desperadoes sharing our hole. Dimples no longer contained herself but erupted from both ends, sprouting tears like a fountain and poop that filled her pants.

"Ugh. Stupid fish-girl!" Hung opened the hatch and stood up. I helped Dimples out of her underwear, which we threw into a basket of fish, and she sat down with nothing but thin pajamas to protect her from the clammy planks. Still, I felt lucky that Hung hadn't thrown her overboard. I vowed to keep an eye on him but the hour was late and the air in the hole was stuffy. Despite my best intentions, I fell asleep.

Father Dragon soon entered my dreams. This time, He didn't bear me aloft on his smoky breath, but placed me on his scaly back and let me ride him like a dolphin playing in the sea—up and down, into and out of the water, making waves and throwing up white mist—then we dove deep, deeper, to the deepest part of the ocean; into and out of rocky caverns, gliding through coral arches. Some part of me, the non-dragon human part, knew that despite my strong desire to win my crown as Princess of the Sea, I couldn't breathe under water; so I held my breath as long as I could but the deeper we dove, the colder the water got and the harder it pressed against my nose and lips but I wouldn't open my mouth, even to scream, just willed myself to hold on and be quiet and be still until somebody poked me hard in the ribs and I let out my breath with a whoosh.

"Twiggy—wake up! The boat is sinking!" Dimples shook my shoulder. Her pants were soaked to the waist, as were mine. Hung was standing in the open hatch passing bailing buckets to the Hue man. The planks in the bilge had sprung serious leak and the water was getting deeper. Dimples and I climbed out between Hung's buckets, teeth chattering, and the Captain ushered us onto the deck away from the stinky air and rising water. Above us a starry canopy wrapped the boat like a globe, the stars dancing on the rippling surface like fireflies. But the Captain saw our blue lips and hustled us to the engine compartment, where he raised another hatch and told us to find a warm spot away from the oily smoke. This I was happy to do, if only to get away from the knife and gun. We snuggled against a bulkhead and in moments we both fell asleep.

In my dream, Father Dragon bore me from under the sea into the dazzling blue air and spiraled up toward the sun. I enjoyed the warmth until His scales turned hot under my hand—searing pain like my arm was on fire. Still, we were high above the sea and I was afraid to let go, afraid to fall down into the water or up into the sun, afraid...afraid...

I awoke and found myself leaning against the hot engine. I jerked back, rubbing my hot arm with a cool hand. Dimples was still sleeping. I rubbed until the pain became an ache then tried to sleep but engine noise and creaking hull—and now pounding rain along the deck—wouldn't let me. It's funny how after a short time on a moving boat, you get in tune with its rhythms: even small changes grab your attention. Something was happening on deck. I pressed my ear against the hatch and listened intently.

"Where's my son, you son-of-a-bitch!" Was it the Captain? I couldn't tell, but the voice was hopping mad. "You promised!" More shouts—way more people than I ever thought on were aboard, as if the whole village had landed on the deck while I was sleeping.

"Stop—Goddam it—or I'll shoot!" The stranger from Hue?

Explosion—a thousand times louder than any Tet firecracker, made my ears ring like a bell. More commotion on deck. A big splash. This hullabaloo woke Dimples who started to cry, so I pulled her close and cuddled her, still afraid to raise the hatch. We stayed that way a long time. Dimples quieted down and maybe went back to sleep. The engine hummed—didn't slow down or speed up, stop or start—so I assumed that Captain Six was still in charge. Then the boat moved in a different way. The bow went up and down, a little at first, then with jumps so big that I heard water slap the keel. The propellers behind us screamed like angry cats when they bit the air, then growled when they fell back to the water. We began to roll as well as pitch: up, down, left, right, bite the air, bite the sea, again and again. Light flashed through the cracks in the deck followed by rumble, rumble, rumble. I'd heard that noise in the summer monsoon, but never so close, never so loud, never right above my head. The engine started to smoke. My stomach churned. I spewed my last meal into the darkness—it sizzled on hot metal.

This woke Dimples up. Her fingers grabbed my arm and squeezed it to the bone.

# 5

## *Sucker Hole*

With Dimples clinging to one arm, I used the other to crack the hatch, partly to get fresh air and settle my stomach, partly to see if the rest of the boat was still there.

The deck was still heaving but my stomach wasn't, so that was good. The stars were gone and the sea air smelled like rain, so I knew we'd sailed into a squall like the ones Father used to complain about. The Captain was in the pilothouse as if nothing had happened—was the shouting and the gunshot a dream? I shed Dimples' hands like a snakeskin and climbed onto the deck. The Captain frowned at me.

"Why aren't you in your hole?" he asked.

"My stomach hurts," which was true. Puking is not the same as feeling like you might, but either way you don't feel good. That was when I noticed all the others: in the pilothouse, crammed along the gunwhales, wrapped around deck hardware like old rags—dozens of them!—but if they didn't bother the Captain, they didn't bother me. I don't know how or when they got aboard or how I missed them when I was shuffled between stinky holes. Maybe they joined us at the checkpoint or afterward at sea, explaining all the noise, or it could've been when I was asleep—I didn't know and didn't care. I only knew the boat was suddenly loaded to the gills and further hiding, except from the rain, was pointless.

One newcomer took the tiller and the Captain came out and grabbed my arm. He gave Dimples a stern stay put look and she did.

He led me forward and plunked me down on the prow like a figurehead. The wind was bracing and the sea spray stung my face—it felt great. "Hang on!" he yelled, clamping my fingers onto the rail, then left. A sheet of rain passed before he returned to dump a bucket of sea water over my head.

"There," he said. "Now you're a mermaid! You won't stink like vomit. You'll feel better in a minute. When you get too cold, wave one hand and I'll fetch you. Don't try to move by yourself in this weather."

Getting too cold didn't take long. He was barely back in the pilothouse when I cried out and raised my arm whether it was from the wicked wind or the even more wicked monsters I knew were lurking in the white-capped waves, I didn't know. I only knew the black wet hell beyond was worse than hot stink of the hell behind me. A second later I was back in "my hole" and the rain began in earnest. Dimples cringed and I saw the front of her shirt was covered in vomit.

The Captain cursed and got his bucket. Dimples stood in the hatch and pulled off her top. He dredged it through the bucket, wrung it out then tossed it back to her. I helped her dress, but as soon as the blouse was on she screamed, "Mama! Maaamaaa!" I looked at the Captain. His expression showed we were thinking the same thing. He upturned the bucket so it wouldn't roll away and helped us out of the compartment and into the pilothouse where dozens of scared eyes blinked back at us.

In one corner, a figure lay sleeping in a blanket. The Captain turned off the lamp, hung it by the wheel, and without saying a word deposited us next to the figure, lifting a corner of the blanket so we could slide in. The sleeper was a woman: she smelled like one, but she did not smell of shrimp paste, which I knew well—and not like fuel or vomit, either—though she had long-brushed hair and seemed confident enough to sleep in the middle of a storm, so we both cuddled up. No matter who she was, she felt warm and soft and safe. With the boat still rocking like a hammock, we both fell asleep right away.

I opened my eyes onto a gray dawn. The people around us were stirring. I smelled food cooking. I nudged Dimples and said, "Wake up. I'm hungry. Let's get something to eat."

Dimples obliged, pulled back the blanket and screamed. Tears and exhaustion behind her, she now saw the woman was not our mother.

"Hey, hey, hey—" the Captain came over and put his arm around her. "Don't worry about it. You'll feel better after some breakfast."

The sleepy lady groaned and turned over, pulling the blanket tight once we were gone. The Captain took us to the rear of the pilothouse where it was jammed with fishing gear, jugs and boxes.

"Here you go," he said in a low voice, giving us a can of condensed milk to share. "Your mother left this just for you. But don't tell the others. They'll take it away."

"Where's Mama?" I asked.

"I told you not to worry," the Captain said. "Everything will be fine. Just drink your milk and get ready for another day."

I looked at the fuzzy horizon. The sun may have shined above the clouds, but you couldn't tell it from the dark-gray sea.

"Are we out of the storm?" I asked the captain.

"Sucker hole," he said, closing the box where he kept the milk. "That's a patch of calm between the storms. The rain and swells will come back. We won't be out of this for a while."

I looked again and saw no sign of land. The Song Hang delta was obviously far behind us and we were somewhere out to sea—farther, perhaps, than Father had ever sailed. Panic began to fill me and I tried to drown it with more milk. Captain Six saw the fear in my face.

"Don't worry about it," he said like a kindly uncle then returned to his morning chores.

The boat was our whole world for more days than I could count on my fingers and toes. Even at noon, the sky was darker than dusk in the village. Storm cells came and went and we spent most of them huddled with the other passengers jammed in the pilothouse, the driest and safest-feeling place on the boat. We were spared the smuggler's hole in the bilge or a return to the smoky engine compartment because of our growing distance from land. Government patrol boats didn't like bad weather, the Captain said, and the crews felt their duty fade with the distance from their Homeland. We even found our "sea legs," as the Captain called them, and he allowed us to move freely except in the fiercest gales, which usually hit after dark. Who needs nightmares when you've got a typhoon in an ink-black sea?

Our biggest problem was the other passengers. They were a motley crew, to say the least: men, women, kids and teens unused to the sea. More than a few were "Chinese, Vietnamese"; immigrants from China who settled in our country generations before but never learned our language and spoke a dialect all their own. The rest were refugees like us, sent or seeking to find a better life, but a few looked like the hardened criminals our local police arrested or ejected when villagers pointed them out. The third morning at sea, one of these characters spotted Dimples drinking from Mama's next-to-last milk can and stormed through the crowd to take it. Another man intervened and while they wrestled, Dimples dropped the can which ended the fight. Both men fell to all fours and lapped milk from the planks before it could dribble through the cracks.

By the end of the first week not only food and fresh water, but fuel, was running low. The Captain had used more gas than expected running against the wind and the swells kept pulling us off course. This was the first time the Captain himself looked anxious—not scared, exactly, just not in control. The adults on board found relief in prayer not that it did much good, but it was better than feeling helpless. Listening to their pleas, I heard a lot of familiar names: Buddha, Jesus, the Virgin Mary, Quang Am, and some I didn't recognize, like Shiva and Allah. My personal prayer was for Father Dragon to extend his wings a little farther from shore to protect us for as long as possible, to hand us gently to our next guardian, the way a mother passes her baby to the father. Was that too much to ask? I did not want to prowl the depths forever as a sea ghost or even reign over murky waters as Sea Princess—as appealing as that idea had been. I had no idea what Dimples was thinking except that she missed Mama as much as me and wondered when the Captain would make good on his prediction that "everything will be fine."

Believe it or not, our prayers were eventually answered.

# 6

## *Life Ring*

After too many days to count, we finally saw another ship. Everyone rushed to the rail and shouted and waved until the Captain told us to pipe down.

"I don't like the look of them," he said, scratching his stubbly chin. "Could be Thai pirates. They hunt these waters like sharks. They'll kill you for the gold in your teeth. Better give them a wide berth."

"No," another man said, "That's a Chinese junk another fishing boat. Look at the sails!"

We all squinted harder. After a few minutes the new vessel got close enough for everyone to see the battened sails and small red flag with one big and four little stars flying from the stern.

"Okay, not pirates," the Captain announced. "These guys are Chinese from the People's Republic. Maybe they'll help us, maybe they won't, but at least they'll talk to us. They're no friends to Hanoi."

With that he went to the pilothouse, cut the engine, and ran a ragged white flag up our boat's short mast. The bigger boat altered course, dropped its sails and starting a little putt-putt engine of its own before drawing alongside. It did not look like a fishing boat—at least not the kind I remembered from An Hai—though the people on board looked fishy enough.

The sea swells were cooperative, so the crew of the bigger boat threw bumpers over the side and lashed us together. Then what appeared to be their skipper and a couple of others jumped onto our crowded deck. Our Captain bowed courteously and shook the other man's hand. They spoke briefly in a language I never heard then went into our pilothouse. We passengers gathered around to see what we could.

They babbled a few more minutes then Captain Six got out a map. He put his finger on a certain spot and the other captain put his finger on a different spot and they babbled some more, bowed politely, and the Chinese returned to their ship. Moments later the lines flew off, our engine started, and the Captain leaned hard on the tiller. We all grabbed a handhold as our boat pushed off. We were on our way, but God only knew for where.

"Why didn't they give us food and water?" One man asked.

"Didn't have any to spare," the Captain answered, staring at the horizon. "Anyway, he pointed to the nearest Chinese port just is a few hours away—we were headed the wrong direction. Now we're back on course heading north, with just enough gas to make it. So everybody settle down, okay? Everything's going to be fine."

This time I was inclined to believe him, so Dimples and I went to the bow and let the fresh breeze bathe us. Miraculously, the clouds began to part and by the time we made landfall—a pitiful little island with a dock, some houses, and trees—the day was sunny and hot.

Inside the breakwater, the Captain cut our engine and coasted nicely to a berth, where his son, Hung, jumped off the bow and looped a line over a piling. Apparently a foreign boat in this little fishing village was big news, so a small crowd had gathered to greet us—or at least to give us a stare. This neighborly greeting didn't last long. Within minutes a squad of soldiers appeared and the bystanders moved back. Using gestures and a firm voice, but still speaking some unknown tongue, they made it clear that those passengers on the pier must immediately get back aboard.

"Gasoline. Water. Food." The Captain tried to be clear but nobody understood him. Finally the lady Dimples mistook for our mother came to the railing and said to Captain Six, "They speak

English. I was an English teacher before the war ended. I can translate." Then she said something in that queer language.

Faces among the soldiers brightened and the man in charge stepped forward and said in English, "We have gas. We have food. What can you pay?"

"We have dong," our Captain said and the woman translated. The soldier shook his head.

"No, really," he persisted, "what money can you exchange for supplies?"

"That's it. No kidding."

"Then if you want to spend dong, go back to Vietnam."

"Fine," the Captain said. "Give us food and water and fuel and we'll go!"

That brought a laugh all around, but it was getting us nowhere.

"Hey," our translator said to the Captain, "make him an offer he can't refuse. Give him international currency."

The Captain paused then retrieved his handy barf bucket from the deck. He held it up to the woman-translator, who removed a jewel necklace from under her blouse and dropped it in. The man next to her offered his watch, as did the man next to him. Soon the bucket was half-full of rings, earrings, watches, crucifixes of gold or silver or jade. The Captain rattled it next to his ear then held it out to the soldier.

"Here you go," he said.

The soldier laughed, took the pail and shook the Captain's hand. The soldiers stepped back and the villagers formed a line shuttling baskets of food, water pails, and a few rusty drums brimming with pungent fuel. The head soldier stepped into the shade to sort his loot.

While this was going on, Dimples and I looked into the shallows on the far side of the boat. The sea was clear as bath water and we laughed as colorful tropical fish swooped in and out from our boat's shadow to pick bits of seaweed off our hull. I asked Dimples if she wanted to jump in and play with the fish, but she just clung tighter to my leg. I guess not. But the afternoon was getting hot and the sandy beach and shady trees and tidy vegetable gardens around the houses made me think of home and the kinds of things I might be doing if Father and Tiny hadn't flown the coop and none of this had happened. I wondered silently when we would see them again, let alone see Mama and Pudgy and Brat and Fly Swat. I wisely kept these thoughts to myself as they would surely make Dimples cry.

The sun was setting as the last of the provisions came aboard. After assuring that none of the visitors had jumped ship, the soldiers slung their rifles and returned to the village. Hung cast off and our faithful engine, thirst quenched with new fuel, started easily. The Captain in his pilothouse swung our bow gently toward the breakwater and the sea. At this point, a small rowboat approach from the far side of the little bay. It bore two Chinese men with bundles on their backs.

"Hey—wait up!" one shouted in English. Our lady translator told the Captain, who throttled back the engine. The rowboat pulled alongside and the man with the backpack spoke again.

Our lady translator said, "They want to come on board and leave the island. He says they know you're going to Hong Kong and want to defect, like us. He says they have Chinese yuan—you'll need it when you get there. He says they're sailors and can help you run the boat. What do you say?"

Hung didn't wait for his father to answer. He flashed his fish-knife at the defectors. "Tell them that if we wanted to go to a Chinese prison we'd just steal their food and gas! Now tell them to get out of the way or we'll run them over!"

The first Chinese man gave a cry and threw his own small fisherman's knife as hard as he could at our boat. He wasn't a good shot. The little knife just missed my head and clattered onto the deck. I didn't know what he'd do next, so I grabbed Dimples and ducked below the railing. The other passengers hit the deck or ran into the pilothouse.

Our engine revved again. The Captain pulled the tiller hard and threw our wake against the rowboat. The two men cursed as we sped away. Minutes later, we were out to sea with the red sun at our backs. The sky ahead was clear, but I could tell from the Captain's face that something troubled him. He knew something we didn't. A different kind of storm way waiting.

# 7

## *Victoria Harbor*

For the next few days, the weather was fine but the swells and current ran against us. Again, the Captain warned that our fuel was running low. Adrift with no power, another storm would finish us, so the prayers and chants began again.

On the bright side, many of us passengers had become useful sailors. Men and boys took turns clinging to the mast atop the pilothouse, focusing their sharp eyes on the horizon, competing to be first to call, "Ship ho!" or even "Land ho," although nobody really expected it.

Finally, one eagle-eyed woman sunning herself at the stern shouted, "Boat!" and pointed to the east. To us, this call was better than a dinner bell so we all ran to starboard to have a look. Captain Six, always cautious when encountering strangers at sea, began a slow turn toward the speck, now visible to all. Soon the white blur was as big as a house.

"A ship," someone said.

"A warship," said another.

"A British warship," said a third.

It was true. The closer we came, more of us spotted the Union Jack fluttering behind a deck that bristled with guns, missiles, and antennas. Surely we would be rescued—"or sunk," said the stranger from Hue as he eased his hand into his pocket to caress his lucky charm, but who knew which? This started the adult passengers rumbling. After all, they said, the American War ended only four years ago. For twenty years, British and Americans rained death on our Homeland, causing suffering to North and South alike. The Chinese, too, had killed lots of Vietnamese—and just this year, only a month after Tet—a short war that left bitter feelings. Assume no one you meet at sea is a friend, the Captain said, and now I was starting to believe him.

Ponderously, the big white warship slowed, gave way then stopped. Captain Six maneuvered our little boat to the stairs that hung from the warship's side and waited. Some round-eyed, golden-haired men—the first British that Dimples and I had ever seen—gathered at the top then descended the steps in their immaculate white uniforms. Bearing clipboards, boxes, and holstered pistols, they looked like seabirds hovering over a ragged school of fish.

The first thing they did was give a megaphone to our translator, whose name we had learned after China Island was Miss Ha. The loud hailer, as they called it, would help her communicate with their commander who stayed aloof like a king on the upper tiers of his white fortress. Few of us had ever seen so many white-skinned, round-eyed humans in one place at one time, all with golden tans that extended from their crisp white shirts and pleated shorts.

Miss Ha and the British officer exchanged words for quite a while—much longer than it took to strike a deal with the Chinese fisherfolk. Eventually, she turned back to our Captain with the warship's terms.

"The British captain says he'll take us under Royal Navy protection, provided our women board his ship and our men stay put on your boat."

"What?" Captain Six was incredulous, "they want our women?"

"Only the cute ones," Miss Ha continued.

Our Captain glanced up at the Grand British Lord and shook his fist. "No!" he shouted. "I'll scuttle my boat before any Englishman lays a hand on our women!" I could see now where Hung got his temper.

As Miss Ha translated, our Captain told his son to untie the boat. Hung hopped to his task and I grabbed Dimples, wondering how long the British would let us drift until they launched their own armed boat to bring us back or simply shoot the men and take what they wanted.

Before Hung touched a line, however, the British sailors started to laugh. More English blared through their loud hailer and Miss Ha started laughing, too.

"What are you doing?" Captain Six asked indignantly. "What's going on?"

"The British captain says he's only pulling your leg. He says his crew has been on patrol a long time and has picked up many small boats like ours. They're making a joke. He asks you to forgive him. He says he will radio Hong Kong and have them send out a proper rescue boat—the usual procedure. The rescue boat will tow us to Hong Kong Island. He asks me to verify that all aboard seek political asylum, right? All Vietnamese? No Red Chinese?"

Our Captain grunted, then told her to answer yes, yes, and yes to the questions. "Tell them we will comply. And tell them thank you."

Our wait for rescue was a long one. Underway at sea, we could at least stand on deck with a cool breeze on our faces. Tied up to the warship, we baked like turtles on a rock, chasing the shadow of our pilothouse as it inched across the deck. If the big ship's stairway had been on the other side, we could have waited in the shade. To their credit, the gold-skinned British sailors bearing the boxes distributed popsicles to all on board. I knew about ice, but didn't know it came in rainbow colors, or on sticks. Some colors were apparently luckier than others, for the adults grabbed the red and yellow ones first, peeling off the sticky paper and eating them like bananas. The British sailors, though, made sure we kids got our share. Mine was purple, like river whelk. Dimple's ice-candy was green as reeds. They were luscious—but between the hot sun and our thirsty tongues, it was hard to keep them from shrinking to wooden sticks, though we tried our best to make them last. I started to tell Dimples that we should remind Mama to get some colored ice-candy when we saw her next, then decided against it. Who knew when that would be, and the mere idea would start Dimples crying.

Finally, after three or four hours, what looked like a bright blue fishing boat hove into sight. It was fast and noisy and left lots of smoke and spray in its wake. But it was just a little bigger than our boat, so I didn't understand how it could handle the weight of two. Hong Kong Island, whatever that was, must be very near.

The rescue boat drew alongside and I counted only four men aboard, all Chinese, all wearing blue jumpsuits. One came on our boat with a clipboard and nodded politely to the Captain and Miss Ha. Since she was the only one who spoke English, I figured Dimples and I should stick near them if we were to know what was going on—and more important, what would happen next.

The blue Chinese man said something and Miss Ha repeated it into the Captain's ear so quietly I couldn't hear it. When the captain nodded, Miss Ha clapped once to get everyone's attention.

"Okay," she said, "these nice men will tow us to Hong Kong for processing. British authorities will interview each of you and a nurse will give you a checkup. He says to hold still for a minute so he can count us—then you can get comfortable for the trip, which will take a few hours. He says no weapons are allowed in the refugee center, so if you have any, the best thing to do is to dump them into the sea. If they discover you with a weapon, they'll turn you over to Hong Kong police and you may lose your refugee status, so even if it's just a pocket knife, toss it overboard as soon as you can."

As she talked, two other blue-suited Chinese men rigged a line from our bow to the stern of their vessel. Hung tried to help but they motioned him away. He didn't like that this was his family's boat—but he didn't cause trouble. If our new hosts insisted on doing everything for us, why not sit back and enjoy it?

As soon as the count was finished, the chief of the rescue men returned to his own boat and its big engines roared to life. They putted off slowly until the lines went taut then Number 6 fishing boat lurched after them, slowly picking up speed. Some passengers turned to wave goodbye to our benefactors on the warship, but the stairs were already rising and the sailors had gone about their business. Clearly, we were not the first boatload of sunbaked, scared and thirsty Vietnamese cowards and traitors they had seen and we would not be the last. I only hoped the next fisher-captain they netted would appreciate British humor.

For the first time on our long voyage, we could actually relax; but each time I started to doze in the lowering sun, Dimples nudged me—as if my waking presence was her only tie to the world. We were really moving fast now, and it was odd to see the captain leaning against the pilothouse while the tiller moved by itself, our rudder pivoting in free water.

As the sun dipped into clouds behind us, dark mountains rose ahead. Minutes later the mountains sprouted a million lights—brighter than the stars at sea. Closer still, the arms of the mountains eclipsed the lights as our rescue-boat turned to the south, bypassing what some of the older, more sophisticated passengers said was one of the grandest harbors in the world—a great space between Hong Kong Island and the mainland filled with boats and ships of every type—so many you could walk from Hong Kong to China without ever wetting your feet. I found that hard to believe, but just thinking about it was an enchanting way to end our harrowing voyage: one I never asked for and thought would never end.

The rescue boat slowed as we neared the shore and what appeared to be a mass of flotsam and jetsam—old sticks and rags and ropes and wires crammed together to make a dam. Closer in, the driftwood dam took on the shape of a thousand boats—mostly fishing vessels like ours, but some rowboats and speedboats and Chinese-style junks with torn or lowered sails.

Before we reached the dock, though, two small, fast patrol boats—like the ones that prowled the Song Hang River—motored up. The rescue boat throttled back, spun sharply, then eased its lumbering companion—us—to a stop, dead in the water. The patrol boats came alongside and policemen climbed onto our deck. They did not look like the friendly British sailors in white shorts or our helpful Chinese rescuers in jump suits. They looked like police do everywhere: hard-eyed and suspicious.

After giving us a quick check, one officer held out a single apple. Our Captain took it, nodded his thanks to the policeman, then passed it to a passenger, sternly cautioning, "Just one bite, then let the next person have a turn!" That first bite was a big one, the next even bigger, the grabbiest people going first before it made its way to the children. Dimples and I were last. The apple was now just a core but its fragrance was sweet and its juice even sweeter. It was almost dark now, so I had no idea what I was eating, except that after even one small bite I wanted more.

"The sweet taste of freedom!" one passenger said in the dark. We all laughed and for the moment at least, we hoped that he was right. Although we were ready to ditch our sea legs for dry land, the police told us to stay on board until space in the Refugee Center was available. According to Miss Ha's translation, nobody knew quite when that would be, so our wait could be a long one.

Sunrise showed Number Six boat had many neighbors—a seaborn village of waterlogged vessels jammed together in a tangle. These new boats came in all shapes and sizes: from deep-sea fishing boats in good repair and sailing junks rigged in Chinese style to tiny row boats I wouldn't trust in a bath tub, let alone the open sea. Some passengers had already started making friends—or enemies, depending on their reception—leaning over the side and talking with the other quarantined arrivals. Although the boat-police made sure nobody swam to shore or started a motor, they didn't seem to care if we Vietnamese mingled with each other so boat-hopping became the sport of the day. From the veteran fugitives, we newcomers learned a great deal.

First, despite our welcome with ice-candy, speed-boat rescue and one sympathetic policeman's apple, Hong Kong's generosity had run its course. Boat people waiting to be processed were more or less on their own so trading, begging, or stealing food from each other was more than a way to pass the time: for some it meant survival. Fortunately, our immediate neighbors were mostly village folk like us who shared our communal spirit. If somebody had even a pinch of rice or bit of fruit or extra sweet potato or fresh-caught fish, he shared it freely with those who would otherwise go hungry. That was nice, but for others food was money. Unless you had Hong Kong dollars or jewelry or something useful to trade from your boat—tools or nails or a can of pitch to seal your leaks—you might as well make a shroud from the clothes you wore. More than one sickly man or starving old lady, I was told, slipped over the side this way. I did not want my last meal to be a mouthful of sea water.

On the other hand, some floating neighbors were relentlessly cheerful. "Oh, you and your little sister will love Hong Kong!" one kindly lady said from three boats over. "They give you warm clothes and blankets and a steel framed bed all your own. Can you imagine such luxury?" I could imagine it, but seeing it would be better. I could imagine seeing and hugging Mama and even being nice to Pudgy and Brat and giving them a popsicle. But for all I knew, they were still on the far side of the world, living in darkness while I enjoyed "the light of freedom," as that same kind lady described it. But was this really freedom—confined like prisoners in a mass of leaky boats? For that matter, was the sky above still guarded by Father Dragon or were we now too far away? One problem with having time to think about such things is that you end with more questions than answers.

So, as they did at sea, one day melted into another. Each sunrise brought the hope of getting off our little boat and each sunset snatched that hope away. Instead, a new day just brought more boats filled with gaunt and hungry ghosts from the sea. Some of our neighbors—the people who'd waited longest—were fetched by police and went ashore, stepping boat-to-boat until they reached the dock then climbed a long plank onto the pier and we never saw them again. We celebrated their success by looting their deserted boats, which usually contained extra food. On a good day, these leavings made our evening meal feel like Tet without the fireworks. On bad days, we ate scraps while kids moped and adults argued.

On the third day, the weather changed. Gray rain clouds covered the mountaintops and we hunkered down in the pilothouse or in the cargo hold with the fish baskets: locked in solitary confinement with our thoughts, the heavy air pierced only by the distant cries of babies. Dimples, never far from tears at best, passed the afternoon with trembling lips. Still, I vowed to be strong for her. Although neither of us had Mama, she at least had me. Being strong and silent worked best, but occasionally I lied about our prospects and repeated the tales I'd heard on other boats about the good fortune that lay beyond. These little fibs made me feel better; and soon a squad of smaller kids, most of them Dimples' age, began to sit with us and followed me from boat to boat as we scrounged for food. They helped keep Dimples quiet and it was nice to have some company—kids more helpless than me, people who looked up to me for a change and didn't view me as a nuisance or a freak. I suppose that's when I realized that freedom wasn't going be easy, or a gift—like a popsickle from the British—but something sturdier I'd have to fashion for myself.

On the fourth day at anchor—or was it a month?—the policemen returned to take us ashore. This was a joyful, monumental moment for everyone but the Captain.

"Tell them I won't go," he said to Miss Ha. "My job was to get you people out of the country and I did. You paid me, I took you. Now you're here. I only want to go home. My family's in Quang Nam province, not in Hong Kong, not in America. Tell them to let me go!"

As she translated, a Chinese policeman put a hand on the Captain's shoulder: not to comfort him, but to begin guiding him from the boat.

"No!" the Captain pulled away. "I want my boat! It's all I have! They can't take it!"

Hung stepped up as if to defend his father, but for the first time in the voyage, I saw doubt in his eyes—maybe even some compassion. Like the rest of us, he felt so close to freedom that he could taste it.

"Father Captain," he said, "We can't go back. There's no safe way. We have to leave."

Captain Six saw that even if the authorities let him keep his boat, he would have to sail it without his son. It was a bitter pill to swallow. His sad eyes narrowed and he broke down and bawled like a baby. Was this the same man who faced all those perils at sea without flinching and risked everything to bring us to this new world? Of course, it was not. A Captain without a boat is not a captain. Now he was just another refugee—a man with a past but no certain future. He was just like us.

Hung and a policeman helped him onto the next boat, then the next, until they reached the dock. Miss Ha stayed at his elbow, trying to calm him down. "Maybe you can reclaim your boat when we clear customs," she said, though I had no idea what that meant. I was only sure of one thing: we had all seen the last of that creaky old boat and I, for one, was happy to put it behind me. Dimples and I fell in line with the other sunbaked ants until we climbed the plank to the dock.

Behind the dock was a long, low building. The Chinese policemen, all speaking English, shepherded us inside through a big sliding door. It was not a government office or a hospital, as some had guessed, but a huge, humid warehouse with open beams and skylights. Instead of finding blue-suited rescuers or white-clad sailors, we joined a milling mass of Vietnamese men, women, and children, elders and babies, circulating like fish in a barrel: talking, jabbering, laughing and crying. With no instructions from police, we knew we were again pretty much on our own. We stayed in a group and gradually merged with the herd. I couldn't guess the number of refugees around us—it had to be many times the population of An Hai and the most people I had ever seen in one place. Finally, a policeman on the edge of the crowd pointed to some white lines painted on the cement floor and made a sleeping gesture with his hands.

"You better pick your place quick," a stranger said as we shuffled deeper into the warehouse. "The best spots are along the wall—nobody steps on you when they go to the toilet. Anybody sick should stay close to the door. The nurses don't come in farther than that. And you kids—stay close to your parents or you'll be sleeping out in the rain."

Since the passengers from boat Number 6 were the closest thing we had to family, Dimples and I stayed with them as they looked for space. We found it near one corner and staked it out; Dimples and me keeping one paint outlined "bed" for ourselves while bigger families took three or four. I then noticed all the people coughing and sneezing around us—half the refugees seemed to be sick. A pale faced young man in the space next to us was among them. He politely scooted over to give us more room.

"You girls are lucky to have parents," he said. "Don't be fooled by all the cops—they just look out for themselves. To them we're just cabbages." That reminded Dimples that we'd left the boat without breakfast.

"When do we eat?" she asked.

"You get two meals a day," the coughing man said. "The line starts over there. Vietnamese-Chinamen go first, followed by native Viet. Orphans and sick people go last, so if you want a decent helping, get in line quick. If you have a cup or a bowl, bring it. Otherwise they just scoop your serving into your hands to onto some paper. Lunch is rice with pickled cabbage and stewed pork, but get there fast because the pork goes fast. Dinner is rice and sardines. Not fresh," he made a nasty face, "You know, the kind that comes in cans."

No, we didn't know, but Dimples and I would find out.

After a few days in the warehouse, Dimples and I started to feel at ease. Not at home, exactly, but less scared. No longer slaves to the waves and weather, we found we could actually take care of ourselves—eat, sleep, go to the toilet (adults had port-a-potties at the back of the warehouse; we kids had to go outside to pee and poo in the bay), and amuse ourselves without a parent's or even the Captain's permission. Fresh water was precious, so bath time was one bucket in the morning, whose contents we ladled over our heads. I'm sure our lice appreciated it.

With some other passengers from boat Number 6, we began to wander the warehouse looking for familiar faces. We discovered that one kid in three was an orphan like us, so we parentless kids began to hang out, as we'd done on the anchored boats. We shared stories, told jokes, made up songs, played games, picked fights and settled them, made friends and laughed or sulked as the spirit moved us. Nobody told us when to go to bed or to "knock that off" or what to do about anything.

These new allies, and this freedom, paid off right away—especially at mealtime. The coughing man was right: Vietnamese with Chinese ancestry usually went to the head of the line. This wasn't a formal rule, but the guards and custodians seemed to treat them better so nobody got in their way. The only renegades were us kids, who discovered that if we were quick enough, we could zip into line ahead of others, or in the middle of a pack, and snatch as much food as we could carry before staff or refugees could react. Whoever was caught first got a pretty good beating, so we used this to our advantage. Before each meal, we'd take turns being the "suicide diner." That person would charge in line like a kamikaze, grab whatever he or she could then toss it to the rest of us, who'd scatter like roaches. Of course, the volunteer got beat up, but for the rest of us it often made the difference between a meal and an empty stomach.

Eventually, some officials arrived to interview the newcomers—whose numbers increased every day. Slowly, the milling refugees lined up by the food tables and passed down the row of officials who asked questions and jotted things down on paper. Dimples and I and our gang had nothing better to do, so we got in line and waited our turn.

When the person ahead of us finished, Dimples and I stood in front of a fair-faced Englishman with a Chinese civilian beside him. The Chinese man spoke Vietnamese, but in a dialect that was hard to understand. For sure, he was not from our village or even from the Central Coast, but we were able to communicate.

"So, you girls are sisters?"

"Yes sir."

"Name and birthday?"

"Twiggy and Dimples. Our birthday is the same as everyone else's—Tet."

"Are your parents with you?"

"No sir, but I hope we'll find them here."

"What are their names?"

"Mama and Father," The man laughed and I couldn't image how such a stupid person could ever rise to a position of authority. What else would we call our parents? Still, the lump in my throat became a morsel of hope. Dimples managed not to cry.

"I mean, what are their last names?" the translator said.

"What is a last name?"

"What did the other villagers call them?"

"Uncle and Auntie."

The translator wrote something down then whispered to the Englishman and they snickered again. I didn't see what was so funny, but it seemed like a good idea to smile with them.

"Okay," the translator said, "we're finished. You go wait over there with the other kids." He pointed to a gang that was not my own, but it didn't bother me. Only two kids were taller than me and I knew that, in a pinch, I could protect Dimples and handle them. After a long time, Captain Six joined the officials who said something to him. He nodded and called us over.

The Englishman adjusted his glasses and read from a piece of paper while the Chinese man translated. "Good news," the translator said. "Your new father is the captain of your boat. He says he knows your family and took care of you during the voyage. He'll look after you in refugee housing. And of course, you already know your new brother, Hung. You should all get along just fine."

All I could think of was Hung's knife at Dimples' throat in the smuggler's hole plus the quick temper he showed everyone else.

"Oh, by the way," the translator concluded, "the captain will call you by the names of his real daughters back in Vietnam: Dinh and Dong. I'm sure you'll all be one happy family. Any questions?"

I wanted to ask when the next boat left for Vietnam, but wisely kept my mouth shut.

The officer then gestured we move along. Captain led us to the other end of the warehouse where the sneering Hung waited in our family space. The Captain said things would continue more or less as they had on the boat and he would make sure we got food and housing and would help us look for Father and Tiny. It was never clear if Dimples was Dinh and I was Dong or vice versa, but it didn't seem to matter as he never called us that. I think it was just something he wanted the officials to put on paper so his daughters would have an easier time of it if they ever made the trip; that or the fact that sponsored families got out of Hong Kong faster than individuals as some of the other passengers mentioned. For now, the Captain dismissed us to get lunch with our friends, which we were happy to do, although Hung pulled us aside as we passed.

"I've got your number," he said menacingly. "Just remember, I saved your butts more than once on the boat. As long as you're in this family you'll do what I say or else."

"We have our own family," I said meekly, pulling Dimples closer. "We won't be here forever."

"Well, your father is whoever the police say he is, so if you give us trouble, you'll get trouble. The guards beat-up people every day or drag them off to prison so just do what you're told and maybe, just maybe, you'll see your family again. Until then, my father is your father and that makes me the boss of you, so don't ever forget it."

As we hot-footed it to the lunch line where our gang was saving our place, I told Dimples, "What a jerk!"

"Yeah, Hung's a real fart face!" she replied, so that became his family nickname.

When we got to the line and I told the other kids what had happened, half were jealous and half was as disgusted by the arrangement as we were. They were particularly outraged that our nicknames, which we'd always worn with pride, had been ripped from us like a pocket from an old shirt.

"As long as we're together," Cockroach said, "we'll go by the names given to us under Father Dragon."

"That's right," Fish Sauce agreed. "Twiggy and Dimples forever!"

"Forever!" Crab said.

"Forever!" Rat Face said and nudged his brother, Little Penis.

"Yeah, forever!" LP added.

Shrimp Paste, the newest member of our gang—a tag-along girl younger even than Dimples and a genuine orphan who spoke so little everyone at first thought she was mute—finally said, "The people on my boat ate my baby brother."

That killed our appetite for the moment, but as the tallest kid in the group, I put a motherly hand on SP's shoulder.

"Then let's promise each other: nobody born under Father Dragon will ever be eaten again."

We all made our fists the hub of a wheel then broke as the line moved forward. Lunch, after all, is lunch.

Like good daughters, we started and ended each day with our new "family," though the time in-between was our own. The worst part of our pretend family life was listening to the dull, odd-ball stories the Captain told us at bed time so that we could share at least a few of his nostalgic memories. Our real life we lived with our gang so Dimples and I were never bored. The best day was Sunday—visitor's day—when local church groups came to the camp to convert us to their religion. Listening to their sermons may seem worse than hearing the Captain's old family stories, but trust me, it wasn't.

"God wants you to have nice things," the nun or deacon or priest would say, then give us gifts like toys, candy, chewing gum, or new clothes, all donated by their parish or sent from America. We each got a Bible, too, although none of us could read English, so they told us what it contained: stories of Jesus and Mary and heroes from a time so long ago in a land so far away that they seemed even more fantastic than the tales we'd heard as toddlers of Quang Am and the heroic Trung sisters who saved Vietnam from the Chinese.

As soon as the missionaries left, we opened shop and sold or traded our church goods to the other kids and adults who missed out. I once made the mistake of showing a pack of gum to Hung—or "Fart Face" as Dimples and I now called him, although never to his face—while I was chewing my first stick. He grabbed a piece like he owned it and told me that if I wanted to blow bubbles, I would have to swallow it first.

I did what I was told then my eyes got big when he laughed. "You idiot! Now your guts will stick together and you'll die. Bet you didn't know that, did you, Sister Twiggy?"

I ran around a few minutes trying to vomit until Cockroach, my second-in-command, saw me and asked what happened. I told him and he laughed, too, then he took pity on me.

"Forget about it," he said. "Fart Face was trying to scare you. Just go outside and sit over the water until you poop it out."

I followed his advice, hoping I wouldn't blow a big bubble from my butt in the process, but everything came out alright. I felt like a big moron for believing Hung but Cockroach assured me that it was worse to be a liar than a dumbbell. Still, I made it a point to keep even further away from Fart Face in case he tried such tricks again.

After a few more weeks, a guard announced at lunch that the Green Bus is coming. I asked the Captain what that meant and he said some of us would be moving from the warehouse to refugee housing, and that his family's—our family's—name was on the list. Normally, this would've meant little to Dimples and me, so used had we become to obeying his orders about this and that. Now, it felt like the Green Bus was going to take us away from our true family: the gang I had created in the Center. Despite myself, my eyes began to water.

"Don't worry about it," the Captain said in his usual way. "Refugee housing is better than this dump. You'll get a real bed and more food and have the freedom to move around. Besides, it takes time to find a sponsor. We may have to move several times. That'll give you time to find your family. Everything will be fine, just wait and see."

The Captain was right about that last part: I would have to see for myself. I gathered my few belongings, which now included some trade goods left over from the nuns, combed the tangles out of Dimples hair, then said goodbye to my crew and joined my paper family in line just as the bus pulled up.

The bus ride was my first real glimpse of Hong Kong and a view of Victoria Harbor. The stories had been right. It stretched between the island and the mainland and was filled with so many boats that we could have walked to Kowloon, the first town on the mainland, without ever getting wet. We passed through canyons of high-rise buildings made of concrete, steel, and glass—but viewed from such a distance that I imagined the people living in them must be as small as mice. Leaving the city, we climbed a steep hill on a winding dirt road that more than once made my stomach rise to my throat.

As the sun set across the bay, we arrived at our second camp which, despite the Captain's promise, was no more impressive than the first. Set on a shallow knoll overlooking a school, it was a low-slung concrete building with one floor above ground and a second in the basement. We filed off in an orderly fashion and an officer told us to squat in place, put our hands over our eyes and hold our breath, which we did, then another man with a big jug attached to a hose and wand walked up and down the line spritzing us with a liquid that smelled like perfume and gasoline. After that, they told us to stand and roll up our sleeves, if we had any, and a nurse went down the line poking us with needles. A couple of kids screamed but they were not in my crew, so I ignored them. To set an example for Dimples, I took my shots without complaint, which gratified the nurse and encouraged her to take a closer look at my scabby scalp. "Hmmm," she said then carried on.

When the spraying and poking and screaming were done, the officer ushered us into the building which on closer inspection now looked less like a residence and more like a prison, which is exactly what it was. Armed guards were posted at the vault-like entrance and the long corridors that stretched out in both directions smelled like pee. With no further ado, custodians in white clothing and police in blue uniforms led us down one endless hallway, stopping now and then to open a heavy door and admit a family or two, depending on size, into a small room before locking the door behind them. Ours was a similar room—really more like a cell whose single window began at the shoulder-height of a man. Besides the four of us in the Captain's "family," another family of four and a third with three members were admitted and checked off the policeman's list: eleven people in an unfurnished, cement floor room designed, at best, for a couple of inmates.

"What is this place?" the father of another family asked the Vietnamese-speaking custodian.

"A hospital," the custodian answered.

"Then why the armed guards?"

"A hospital for the mentally ill, the criminally insane. The Refugee Center is full and it's the only place that had space. Trust me, you're better off here. Safer, too. That's why we keep the doors locked. If you need to get out, to go to the toilet or see a doctor, just bang on the door or shout. Someone will come. Otherwise, you keep the same schedule as the convicts, two hours a day to eat a meal and exercise then back to your cell. So make yourselves comfortable. You won't be here too long."

# 8

## *Queen Rat*

As we had done in the Reception Center, each family staked out its place on the floor. Captain Six and Hung took one corner, as did the other men and their wives, and we kids slept like dogs huddled together in the center. Fortunately, the Captain's spot was near the window, so although the glass was too high for me to see anything but sky, I thought it might have a positive effect on my dreams—or at least make our tiny cell feel less like the smuggler's hole on the boat.

Our first two-hour break from the cell was a real eye-opener. While we were left on our own in the warehouse, the guards here kept a close eye on everyone, since the convicts and refugees mingled and we found out pretty quick that nobody—Hong Kong thugs serving their time or the guards who watched them—appreciated our presence. It's one thing to be fish in a barrel, another to be scum at the bottom of the pond! When a we didn't obey a guard fast enough, even though the command was in English or Chinese, they'd elbow us or jerk us by the arm. Gradually we learned which guards were sticklers and which could care less, and this knowledge often saved us from welts and bruises. Some of the teenagers, though, resented the prison atmosphere and talked back. These older kids were named troublemakers and in some cases, rough treatment turned into beatings. The biggest lesson they learned was not to get caught.

Another problem was the fights that broke out everywhere. At first they were for good reasons: someone poached on your turf or stole something from your cell when doors were open. Then once families got to know each other, fights broke out over girlfriends and boyfriends, old feuds from the Homeland, even the way someone dressed or combed his hair. And once parents and grandparents joined in, these conflicts turned into vendettas that lasted for weeks—another reason police took all knives, screwdrivers, and fish-gaffs away as soon as we entered the system. Eventually, some families stopped talking to each other altogether except to curse or shout.

Since Dimples and I had limited time to exercise and it began to rain a lot, the window of our cell became our window on the world. The problem was that the bottom of the sill was way higher than our eyeballs, so one day I told Dimples to climb on my back. I made a table for her on my hands and knees, but she was still too short; so I stood with her piggy-back then had her hang from the window ledge while she found a foothold on my shoulders. During our first attempt at this, the Captain asked what we were up to.

"Trying to bust out?" he chuckled.

"We heard the school bell and children laughing outside," I explained. "We just want to see what's going on."

"Curiosity killed the cat!" Captain Six said as he took Dimples on his shoulders and gave her a good look. Whatever she saw left her speechless.

"Okay, now it's my turn!" I whined.

But Dimples started to cry when her feet hit the floor and the Captain said, "Okay, you both get to peek for a count of ten then it's the other girl's turn. Deal?"

So in ten second bursts, I studied the little valley at the foot of the knoll where students in white shirts and blue skirts (for girls) and blue slacks (for boys) milled around for what the Captain explained was recess: like our exercise period, it was a time when students take a break from class to stretch their legs and socialize on the playground. I was tired of prison life and wanted badly to join them. I was sure that I could organize the kids at recess at least as well as I'd led my crew in the warehouse.

After that, Dimples and I planned our day around the school bells—just like the kids below. After we woke up, we played noisily until the first bell rang, then behaved seriously until the bell for recess sounded, then played noisily in our space and repeated the pattern during our two-hour break, eating our sober meal then running hog wild with the other kids in the sunshine and fresh air. By the time the last school bell rang, we'd had a busy day.

The discipline of our pretend school taught us the finer points of prison life. For example, little currency came into the compound besides worthless Vietnamese dong, so we needed a new kind of money. Wealth and status went to people with useful things, even if they had to make those things themselves. Drinking cups were prized, so people found ways to cut the tops from soda cans and grind down the edges to make them smooth for sipping. This became such a popular pastime, that we were often kept awake at night by the noise of aluminum scraping on the cement floors of adjacent cells. Rubbed just right, this industry produced colorful cups and bowls and the more of them you had, the greater your status on the cell block—though this pastime was mostly for adults.

We kids had other measures of wealth. Every soda bottle cap and every tab on a pop-top can went straight into somebody's pocket, adding to their family's treasury; and if you got too many for your pockets, you wore them around your neck or your waist on a string. This show of wealth, of course, made the kid wearing them a target for bullies, sneak thieves, or con artists, so Dimples and I kept our bankables stashed under our shirts. Strangely, this currency probably stopped as many fights as it started. It gave kids a better way to exchange goods and services than theft or fighting, and even skinny little girls like us could become queen-of-the-corridor if we collected enough.

So our prison-asylum became a world of its own. Other camps, we discovered, let their inmates leave the premises and go to market or look for family in neighboring camps. A few of these lucky people made their way to our facility after dark when the lights were shut off and the guards were either asleep or too busy watching the real convicts to notice. These visitors smuggled food, new clothes, candy and cigarettes through the window gaps for their family and friends. No one ever came for us.

Disappointed that even after many weeks none of my old crew showed up in my new building, Dimples and I made new friends. But the prison kids were boring. Most lived in cells with their original parents, brothers and sisters, even their aunts and uncles. They had no shortage of friendly faces and familiar voices to comfort them when things got tough, which they often did at night when crazy inmates howled and fights broke out in the locked-down cells. And, as with any village, death was a frequent visitor. Several times a week dark angels called, taking some granny or grandpa through disease or old age. Even young people wounded in fights or by beatings from guards felt the beat of their wings, as did otherwise healthy men and women who cut their wrists or drank poison in despair. Some nights, the wailing of the survivors was worse than the shrieks of the sick and dying.

One evening just before lock down, a young man from our cell fell down, twitching and foaming at the mouth. The guards swarmed around him and a few minutes later, an ambulance appeared at the front of the building, lights flashing. The medics put the man on a stretcher, slid him into the back, and drove off. We returned to our cell and Dimples and I took our spot on the floor, as we usually did after a busy two hours of trading in the yard, but the episode with the young man had upset me and I knew that it scared Dimples. Very much unlike herself, she refused to eat the candy we had taken as part of our haul.

A few hours later, when it was dark and we were thinking of sleep, the ambulance returned and the young man was handed over to his mother. Far from looking like an invalid, he glowed like an angel—as if he had seen the face the Buddha.

"It's like one big diamond," he said smiling as he passed us in a daze.

"What's like a diamond?" his mother asked.

"The city beyond the school. The glass towers behind the hills. Pictures made out of lights. Words written in colored glass. Great, heavenly lights of every size and shape. It's a miracle. One big diamond in the night!"

This weird report shut his mother up. Dien cai dau, Hung muttered, "cracked in the head." If he was nuts, he was at least in the right place. The young man suffered two more seizures, bringing with them two more rides in the ambulance, until the guards decided he was faking it to get out of the facility. Dimples and I believed him, though, and we plied him with soda and candy just to hear more about this fabulous Land of Diamonds. We never discovered if it was real or imagined, but it made a great story and in a way, it gave us hope.

When the newest hot commodity—rubber bands—hit our refugee community, Dimples and I were ready to corner the market. These were prized by adults as well as kids, who used them to hold back long hair and hold together everything else—pencils, chop sticks, even collections of soda-can drinking cups. Children wore rubber bands on their wrists and ankles like jewelry, or joined them into chains to make long jump ropes. Here again we saw a way to profit. The littler kids just wanted to play, not collect rubber bands for status, so Dimples and I made our own triple-thick rubber jump ropes—high quality stuff!—and held each end while these kids paid the going rate for a certain number of jumps. Those who had nothing to barter paid their debts by doing us favors, like keeping lookout for the guards if we got too noisy. If a kid was strong enough, we let them settle by carrying Dimples and me around the yard or down the corridor piggy-back, like a princesses in a carriage. All this didn't make us miss Father, Tiny, Mama, Pudgy, Brat, and Fly Swat any less, but it did make our current situation more tolerable. We were pack rats with easy pickings and were learning to feather our nest. As for me, it was good to be queen—at least as long as it lasted.

# 9

## *Land of Diamonds*

One day Captain Six announced happily that we would be moving out of our hell-hole and into another camp. "This one will be different," he said confidently. "This one is special. It's the final place they keep you until you have a sponsor."

Dimples was thrilled and clapped her hands, but I wasn't so sure. We had moved before and it ended in disappointment. Truthfully, I was secretly angry with Father for putting us through all this. If he had just waited until the family could go with him, Dimples and I would've been spared the perilous boat ride, encounters with high seas profiteers, the "ghost boats" clustered in Victoria Harbor, endless weeks of living stranger-upon-stranger in the warehouse camp, then more risks and struggles in prison-asylum—this fortress of insanity that held us hostage to the promise of freedom. Was all that really better than minding our own business and putting-up with government rationing, nosy neighbors, and occasional visits from the police? I was beginning to doubt Mama's wisdom in sending us on this endless trip to nowhere. We'd seen lots of strange sights and learned lots of new things, but I could've gotten all that from Mama's lullabies and stories. What started off as a big gamble was starting to feel like a big mistake. Still, I kept my mouth shut. I went along with the program.

Part of our preparation to move meant applying the lessons that we'd learned. I told Dimples to stop selling the goods we ourselves liked to eat and drink and start trading away prison currency—bottle caps, aluminum tabs, lidless soda cans, and rubber bands—for things more useful anywhere, like underwear, shirts and blankets.

The time between the captain's news and our actual move was hardest. We weren't the only refugees thinking about the future, so trade goods dried up fast as people began to horde. With no business to conduct, no games to play, and most of the refugee kids now sticking close to their families, Dimples and I just hung around the cell, taking turns staring out the window and sleeping. If naps were an Olympic event, we'd have won gold medals.

Finally the big day arrived. Even before the first school bell rang, guards passed down the hall unlocking each door, telling everyone to file out for roll call at the entrance—the busses would arrive in an hour. The remarkable thing about all this was that the guard actually smiled at us. There had been a fall-off in corporal punishment, let alone beatings, throughout the facility—at least among the refugees—as families stuck closer together, afraid to do anything that might spoil their parole. In truth, the guards were as happy to see us go as we were happy to leave, even though they knew that after our cells had been emptied they would be filled again with a new load of confused and bitter refugees. But that was their problem, not ours.

When it was finally time to go, we boarded a different green bus. This one had no seats and the sides were open and covered with chained link, obviously vehicles used to transport prisoners—or poultry. The guards kept packing people on until we stood pressed together like sardines with our few belongings strapped between our feet. Yet no one complained. Nobody wanted to be kicked off for bad behavior. We were cooperative, not stupid.

The bus took us down the winding road then accelerated onto a highway filled with fast-moving cars, including red double-decker busses jammed with people headed toward their future. We studied them the way caged chickens watch buyers at the market.

The bus weaved through more valleys of high-rises until we exited onto a narrow road that led to a wide stretch of flat land. More gates opened—chain link this time, with barbed wire on top, but no warehouse, no insane asylum; just acres of dirt and long sheds made of tent-topped corrugated steel laid-out wherever there was space. The people cramming the dirt streets looked at us with curious faces, maybe even a trace of hope. Some even waved. Half wore our traditional black pajamas or white blouses, which made me even more homesick. It was as if every village on the Central Coast had been swept up and deposited in this enormous chicken farm.

The sun was high above our head by the time we disembarked and answered roll call. Then the prison-asylum guard got back on the bus and drove away. More people with clipboards—and more police in pale blue uniforms with badges, nightsticks, and holstered guns—met our group. Bystanders closed-in. They studied our faces and we studied theirs.

Sadly, the new camp's hospitality, such as it was, ended at the gate. We newcomers were told to squat where we stood and wait for our barrack's assignment. We were told that would take a few minutes, but those minutes turned into hours, all of them in the sun. It was so hot and dusty, in fact, that we dried up like raisins: nobody could pee—and we were there all afternoon. Finally, some of our companions began calling to residents as they walked by. A policeman came up and told us to be quiet. I guess he was afraid we'd start another riot which, we had heard from visitors to our asylum, was not uncommon in that camp.

Finally, close to sundown, custodians came with bottled water and big pots from which they heaped steamed rice and chopped lunch meat onto mess plates—a real feast at this point. While we ate, we were shocked to see refugees leaving the camp just by showing an identification card at the sliding gate. If this was the beginning of freedom, it tasted better than our unexpected dinner!

We watched the liberated prisoners come and go with fascination and envy. One middle-aged man sweeping the road gave us a quick smile, flashing a row of gold teeth.

"Father!" Dimples shouted, but the broom-man turned away just as I looked. He swept, turned again, and I saw it too.

"Father!" I called and stepped forward but the guard steered me back.

"There will be plenty of time to meet camp people later," he said.

Then the broom-man looked at us again. The gold teeth were unmistakable. It was Father! But why didn't he return our greeting? Why didn't he run up and sweep us into his arms? Why did he care so much about that stupid road? It didn't make sense.

Dimples and I kept squawking and waving our arms until the guard came back and poked us gently with his night stick.

"Shhhhh," he put his fingers to his lips so we shut up. After a few fatherly glances, the road-sweeper walked away.

Was he really Father or just an illusion—a man or a ghost? At this point, we couldn't guess. I only know that as soon as I saw that half-forgotten gold-toothed smile, the flame of rage I was fanning inside me instantly blew out.

As night fell, more custodians arrived to show us to our quarters. The buildings got no better the further we moved into camp. Each long hut had a central corridor from which sleeping areas containing six metal-framed bunk beds were arrayed on either side. These were barely big enough for one person, even small people like Vietnamese, but two to four of us were assigned to each, so Dimples and I took one lower bed and Captain Six and Hung the upper. This put us closer to the rats and mice that, we would discover, cruised the dirt floor after lights went out. But at least we now had the bed the nice lady in the boat-jam had promised, and with the blankets we brought with us, whether folded on the sleeping platform or hanging from the upper bunk for privacy, made it actually seem like home. Still, I reminded myself not to get used to it. Tomorrow we might see another wire-cage bus.

Just before lights out, two matrons came through the shelter giving kids like us powdered milk. It seemed like years since I'd tasted milk on the Captain's boat, so I ate the powder raw while Dimples waited for the second lady with cups and hot water.

That first night, Dimples complained that our bed was too warm (the upper berths caught better breeze) so we bailed and took our chances with the rodents on the floor. Actually, the rats and mice weren't as scary as the scuttling sound they made. As long as you brushed any crumbs from your clothes before you went to sleep, they never tickled you with their whiskers. The same was true in An Hai, where the river rats climbed the poles as soon as our oil lamps went out. Actually, I think the rats had more to fear from us than we from them. Head lice, ticks and fleas like a warm, furry host and with my hair not yet grown back and thin pajamas, I was neither.

The next day we explored the camp. A few of the shacks had been converted to classrooms where transients like us could learn English or Chinese, but both languages were too complicated for kids who'd never been to school, so we looked for adventure elsewhere. Mainly, we looked for the road-sweeper who might be Father, but the camp was filled with such people. We followed the inside fence for what seemed like miles until Captain Six spotted us and asked if we were trying to escape. Before we could answer, he laughed and said we weren't prisoners—the fence was mostly to keep the locals out. He said the poor Chinese who lived in Hong Kong resented our free housing and government rations. If ours was a life to be envied, I thought, the locals must have it tough.

"Anyway," Captain said, "tomorrow you'll get a picture ID. You wear it around your neck and can use it to leave and re-enter the camp."

"Just like that?" I asked.

"Just like that. You can even go into town. Everyone here are encouraged to start taking care of themselves so you'll be self-sufficient when you're resettled."

We hustled back to our compound with this news and struck-up a conversation with some kids who had been here awhile, trading the remains of our asylum candy for tips on where to go and what to do once we got our pass to the Land of Diamonds. The picture they painted of camp life wasn't as rosy as we expected. Since camps like these were the last stop before sponsorship, nearly everyone got dumped there—including people the authorities simply wanted to get rid of: petty criminals, gang members, and political radicals—some of them violent. The guns and clubs the camp police carried were not just for show! Drug-dealing was rampant and rapes were as common as riots which, one kid said, sometimes got out of hand. That led to occasional mass breakouts followed by retribution by the guards, most of which were Chinese who already had no love for Vietnamese. This gave Dimples and me a lot to talk about when we returned to our bunk, and we chattered until Captain Six asked from above if we could please give him and Hung a little peace and quiet. We did, but not for long.

Just as we settled on the dirt floor, a man's bare feet appeared by my head. They were dirty and smelly and in the dark, I had no idea who they belonged to until I heard the Captain say from his top bunk, "Oh, there you are! Well, it took you long enough to find us!"

I looked up and saw four brass teeth glinting back at me in the darkness. I sprang up and resisting the urge to hug Father's waist, bowed respectfully. Dimples awkwardly did the same.

"Whoa there," his half-forgotten voice was low and rumbly, as if he was afraid of being heard. "What a pair of polite daughter's I have!" A fisherman's calloused hands caressed the top of our heads affectionately.

"It's a good thing you came," the Captain said, "your girls are driving me nuts!"

"Thanks for taking care of them," Father said then nudged our shoulders, "Tell the Captain thank you for his troubles."

We mumbled something appropriate, but we couldn't take our eyes off Father.

The Captain asked, "Why didn't you come over and talk to us when we arrived?"

"Couldn't. I broke curfew the night before and they had me pushing broom. They told me I couldn't talk to anyone but the custodians for three days. I shouldn't be talking to you now, but I just had to see the girls and let them know I'm here and happy to see them."

"Where is Tiny?" Dimples asked. "When will he visit us?"

"He's in the hospital," Father answered, "but don't worry—it's just an ear infection. My punishment ends tomorrow and I'll take you to see him."

Father glanced down the corridor to make sure no custodians or matrons were coming then ducked into our lower bunk. "How are things at home?" he asked the Captain.

"Bad," the Captain answered. "Worse than bad. Most of the textile mills are closed and most of the rice goes to the Army. When I left, the people were living off pig bran. To tell you the truth, the pigs have it better than us. At least they can eat garbage."

"How is my wife?"

"She's doing okay. Got in trouble with police after you left but they let her go. That's when she decided to put her kids on my boat." He waited for Father's reply but there was none, so the Captain continued, "Hey, what do people do around here?"

"We work."

"Fishing?"

Father laughed. "I wish! No, they don't trust us with a boat. They truck-in manufactured parts for us to assemble—you know, we put toys and transistor radios together, things like that. Whatever the factories need."

"Do we get paid?"

"You bet. Good money, too—Hong Kong dollars you can use to buy anything, or save for foreign exchange once you find out where you're going. I save most of mine. You'd do best to do the same."

The men talked like this most of the night. Father was on probation, so he had to sneak back to his bunk in the adjoining camp before he was missed; but once you had your ID, nobody cared where you went as long as you were back in your camp before curfew. Even freedom, we were learning, had its rules. We went to sleep to Father's voice, washing over us like waves on a beach. To my surprise, I didn't dream of Father Dragon; just our rickety old stilt-house and the sweet taste of Tet pudding.

The next morning we got our ID badges and after that, we left the camp. It felt strange but exhilarating to walk out a gate with no guard or custodian or matron ahead or behind us—only Father, the Captain, and Uncle Six, who lived in Father's camp. It was the closest thing we'd had to a family reunion since Tet.

A big local market lay just outside the gate, so we shopped our way through it using Father's HK dollars. We bought a gift for Tiny—some star fruit and American candy before boarding a double-decker bus for the district hospital. This time the bus wasn't free, so Father had to pay as we got aboard. They say freedom has a price and I guess this was part of it.

After a ride through jammed streets (we could've made better time by walking!) we got off at the hospital. Checking his new wrist watch—the first one I'd seen Father wear, An Hai fishermen needed only the moon and stars to tell time—he said, "We have to hurry. Visiting hours are almost over."

We walked fast down the polished corridor, passing nuns, nurses and doctors in white coats with rubber tubes around their shoulders. Glowing in the fluorescent lights, they all looked like angels in a marble palace. I almost envied the patients who stayed there.

"Is this what's it's like inside a diamond?" Dimples asked.

"No, stupid," Seeing Father made me think of Pudgy, so as the family's resident big sister, I felt obliged to act like one. "It's what it's like inside a hospital!" I couldn't believe we were going to see Tiny!

At a desk beside the hallway, a nun said in Vietnamese, "Sorry, children are not allowed in the wards."

This seemed strange, since Father said Tiny was being cared for in the "children's wing" of the hospital and who had a better right to be there than kids, but we didn't argue. Uncle Six took us outside until Father and the Captain returned a short time later. As we turned to leave, a small face appeared in the door window of our brother's ward.

"Tiny!" I recognized him at once, waved, and he waved back. A nun appeared behind him and his grinning face disappeared so

Father led us back to the street. Except for the stranded branch of our family, I now knew that everyone cast to sea was all right. While that knowledge should've buoyed by step, I felt heavier as we neared the bus stop. Not only was I starting to sound like the oldest, most responsible sister, I was starting to feel like one inside.

That evening, after Father and Uncle Six went back to their camp, Dimples and I sat with some other kids outside our shelter. We enjoyed the cool night air and counted the numberless stars above Hong Kong. I wondered if Mama, Pudgy, and Brat might be counting those same stars at that very moment, maybe from the deck of a boat, maybe in America.

"What's the moon made of?" Dimples asked.

"That's a silly question," I answered. "It's the big diamond in Father Dragon's crown and all the stars are jewels around it."

"How come you know so much?" Dimples was understandably amazed.

"She doesn't know anything," a boy's voice came from the darkness. All we kids looked up. It was Tiny—a skinny thirteen-year old with a hospital go home bag under his arm: medicine drops and cotton balls for his ear, he later explained.

"Tiny!" I jumped up to hug him, as did Dimples. The other kids stood respectfully, which was kind-of odd unless Tiny was their crew leader, as I had been in other camps. Maybe that talent ran in the family.

Tiny explained how he'd been discharged later that afternoon and made his own way back to camp. Tiny had always been like that—not exactly impatient, just independent and liked doing things his way. Once he made up his mind about something, it was best to go along with him. We talked a while about his own adventures at sea and in the camps and in town, plus the astounding things he'd learned from the Catholic nuns in the hospital, until it was time for him to join Father in the neighboring compound. The rest of us went to our bunks.

Early the next morning, Tiny dropped by to "take us to breakfast"—not in the camp mess line, but downtown, as he called it: into the heart of the Land of Diamonds.

Joined by some kids from his crew, we began at the market beyond the gate. "Want some milk?" Tiny asked. "The tofu vendor gives you free soybean drinks. The butcher shop over there makes great barbeque. If you want something stronger, I can get you into the liquor stores."

"Sounds like you're king of the mountain!" I said with genuine admiration.

"What's a king without a kingdom?" he smiled. "Look, there's really nothing to it. The soybean guy gives us soy milk because he feels sorry for refugees. That touch is easy. The butcher shop is tougher because meat is expensive, so go there near the end of the day when he's got cuts that will go to waste. Liquor stores are the easiest. They're always full of people, so you can take what you want as long as you're careful. They've got lots of snack food, too. I always take a few of Father's HK dollars when I go out, but I only spend 'em if I get caught. Fair is fair, after all."

I felt like I should be memorizing this, but I wasn't sure all that sneaking and shoplifting was building the good karma we'd need to get to America, so I decided that Dimples and I would just watch the master and participate if the vibrations felt right. The second night after Tiny got back, we were glad we waited.

Tiny was holding court in the space between the shelters when an ambulance pulled up, lights flashing, and stopped at our shed. A few adults gathered around, including Father who had been visiting the Captain. After the adults spoke with the driver, Father waded into our gang and grabbed Tiny by the arm, yanking him into the ambulance which drove them both away. I had no idea what was going on, but suspected it had something to do with the contents of the go home bag Tiny brought from the hospital. This also showed us a side of Father I'd almost forgotten—the gruff nature with which he was born. When he was around authority—policemen in An Hai, river patrolmen on his boat, guards and custodians in the camp—he was so humble and apologetic it was almost embarrassing. When the encounter was over, though, he took out his anger on his family, reminding us loudly and sometimes violently who was in charge. It didn't happen often, but it happened. Maybe it was that little piece of Father inside me and Tiny—even inside Pudgy—that made us take charge and lord-over other kids. Though I was too scrawny to physically threaten anybody, Tiny and Pudgy weren't.

When the ambulance was gone, Dimples and I scurried back to our bunk and found Captain Six and Hung fast asleep. (Fart-Face Hung had started sleeping in our lower berth, since we never used it and he felt he could muscle us around as he pleased when the Captain wasn't looking.) That night, though, sleep did not come easily, even on the floor.

The next morning, Father came by to take us to breakfast (regular breakfast, in the mess line) and told the Captain, "Can you believe it? Tiny sneaked out of the hospital! Pronounced himself cured and helped himself to some medicines on the shelf. I don't think he knew what he took. He just wanted more stuff to trade in camp."

"Maybe he just wanted to see his sisters," Captain Six said, always willing to give people a break.

"Maybe. But he made me lose face in front of the guards and doctors. Now heaven help us if we get sick. He won't get away with it. Just wait until he gets back!"

"Well, don't be too hard on the boy," the Captain said, "Keep your temper and you'll keep your friends—that's what my father always said."

This time, at least, Father took the Captain's advice. A few days later when Tiny was discharged the right way, the ambulance drove him back to camp and his pals—and his family—greeted him like a hero. Father was so pleased that he invited everyone in earshot to a bus ride into town for a banquet of roast duck and roast pig. Everyone had a fine time although the big meal cost Father just about all his savings. If freedom wasn't free, we learned, then neither was family pride.

# 10

## *Death of a King*

It wasn't long after his return that Tiny reverted to his old ways. He often took Dimples and me out of camp before mess-hall breakfast, knowing there would be few inmates or custodians prowling beyond the gates at that hour.

A new haunt he'd discovered—much to the delight of his young fisherman's soul—was the dock beyond the market where morning boats delivered their nighttime catch. At first he relied on our refugee status to cadge a few handouts, but the Chinese fishermen only parted with mealy baitfish—unfit for humans unless you were really starving. Finally, Tiny told us just to say what the Chinese beggars said: Bi ngo yat tieu, which we tried to copy in their now familiar Hong Kong accent. This yielded better results, but when the Chinese kids informed the fishermen that we were Vietnamese imposters, the palm of charity closed into a fist and the captains chased us off of the docks. This did not deter Tiny in the slightest.

"To hell with them," he said. "Let's get the fish ourselves." So we did. We scampered over the piers and along the stony shore looking for dropped or washed-up fish and each day came home with at least a few that filled our small bellies and increased Tiny's status as king of the mountain—or at least our little hill. Unfortunately, the Chinese kids saw us too and began to scavenge; and outnumbering us ten to one, took over all the good spots. Eventually, we had to choose between spending some of Father's Hong Kong dollars to buy cheap fish at the market or risk returning empty handed. Fortunately, Tiny had a plan for this as well.

His favorite fish-monger was a cross-eyed man who scared Dimples half to death. Tiny was partial to him because with only one eye to watch his stock, shoplifting from him was a cinch. Dimples swore that the other eye was always on her, so she soon quit our breakfast club and took all her meals in the mess line. Father never interfered with any of this. He preferred fresh fish, too—even bait-fish and our scrawniest findings—and once Tiny began frying his "catch of the day," Father tucked-in with the rest of us. In truth, I think the fish-monger knew exactly what was going on and just winked at it. When Tiny occasionally returned empty handed, Father grudgingly gave him a few HK dollars to make up the difference. Once Tiny started buying his fish above board, the cross-eyed vendor always gave him a little extra and made sure that even the smallest fish was fresh.

Night time was the best time for camp residents. Married couples who had money went into town, as did single men and women on dates. If our paperwork was processed any slower, they'd have needed a maternity ward for the compound.

For us kids, it was a different story—but not by much. We tried to do everything the adults did and usually got away with it. We roamed the brightly lit streets in gangs of eight to ten, blending-in with big Chinese families and crowds enjoying the Bright Diamond's night life. Lack of money didn't stop us—not with clever street captains like Tiny to show us the way. Those who wanted cigarettes got them, although one pack lasted a long time since the first owner usually puked his guts out then passed the remainder on to us. The same was true for liquor, which burned going down and even more coming up. When our light-fingered ways caught up with us, as they sometimes did, somebody usually had a little money to pay the shopkeeper—though even working parents like Father were tight-fisted with their cash. Tiny helped us out there as well.

"Look, getting cash is easy," he told us. "First, you wait until a restaurant or bar is about to close. The owners always put their empty bottles out in front to be collected—we just get there before the trash man. Cheap places will spend good money for an empty booze bottle with an expensive label—" and he told us just what brands to look for. As always, American products sold best.

When the pickings were slim—as they were on certain Chinese holidays—Tiny came up with alternatives. Shoplifting was his art and Dimples had her eye on a cute beaded pink purse we just couldn't buy on Father's salary. We passed it every day in the window of a Chinese man's shop, but it was too risky for Tiny to swipe, even if we girls made a distraction. That's when he explained his idea for "trading up" the chain of merchandise. When he had collected several stolen items, he could swap them in for something better. That's how he thought he'd get Dimples her purse, but it sounded too risky for me and despite Dimples' objections, I told him we wanted out. Each family has room for one fox, and Tiny was ours. He could size up a situation, figure out what to do, then had the nerve to do it. I knew these weren't noble traits, but you had to admire his craft—especially since nobody got hurt in the process.

Except once, and it was a lesson we never forgot.

One hot summer night, Tiny tried to organize an expedition into town but Dimples and I and the rest of his crew were too tired so he went alone. We didn't think much of it. He was always getting into something, somewhere, and always came back with a great story. Father and the Captain were in our shelter talking about old times while Dimples and I played on the floor, but given the lack of a tropical breeze, the heat was just too much. We stretched out and nodded off.

Suddenly—one, two, three hours later?—the night watchman clomped into our area, waking us instantly. Two HK policemen followed him, hands clamped tightly on a young teenager. The boy still clutched a beaded pink purse, the price tag still on it.

"That's him, that's the father," the watchman pointed to Father who, white faced, slid from the bunk.

"Shoplifting, theft, larceny—" the guard began running through a long list of charges. He snatched the pink purse out of Tiny's hand and threw it to Father's feet, almost hitting Dimples.

What happened next was a blur. Father's face turned red and he lunged at Tiny. I covered Dimples' eyes because I knew what was coming. Father slapped Tiny once, twice then started beating him with his fists. Tiny screamed and covered his head then fell to the floor, where Father started kicking him. The policemen did nothing. The camp guard did nothing.

Finally Dimples pried my fingers away and shrieked. Father stopped the beating and looked around. I dragged Dimples into the corridor by the arm then out into the starlit night. We waited for more screams, more shouting, but everything went still. A few moments later, the guard and the policemen returned to the front gate with the beaded pink purse. A short time after that, the now-familiar ambulance arrived. The medics rushed in and left with Tiny on a stretcher. The bystanders dispersed into the darkness. Father must have left with them and gone back to his camp—he was not by the Captain's bunk when we returned.

Dimples and I finished the night huddled together on the floor.

Early the next morning, Father came to our room. Dimples was sound asleep, just as I pretended to be. Captain Six was sitting on the edge of his upper bunk, legs hanging over the side. Father greeted him contritely.

"You think I was too rough with Tiny," he framed his question as a statement.

The Captain shrugged and said nothing.

"I had to show them I can discipline my son. I mean, the police were right there. They could've taken him to jail. What chance would he have getting to America with a police record? I did what any father would do. I just didn't know when to stop."

"You almost killed him," the Captain said.

I peeked at Father and saw he was ready to cry.

"I know," he said, and left the room.

Father went into town that morning, mostly to check on Tiny in the hospital but also to make sure the police hadn't filed any charges. I guess he was successful because nobody mentioned the incident again, even when Tiny was discharged. Still, Tiny was different after that. So was Father. Tiny stuck close to camp, going into the local market occasionally to buy fish but seldom going downtown. He showed little interest in Dimples and me and when his adventures and stories stopped, so did the adulation of his crew and the other kids pretty much left him alone. It was as if something inside him had died—not a bad thing when you consider the path he was on, but it still felt like a death in the family.

Father changed his ways too, at least a little. He was kinder to Tiny, as he was to all of us, though we gave him no reasons to lose his temper or lose face. The best you could say about our family life at that point was that it was proper—formal and correct, but never again joyful or spontaneous. Dimples and I had found the father and brother we were looking for, but at the cost of the family we remembered. Once again, we had only each other—two chopsticks that made a pair, two peas in the same pod—and for now that would have to do.

# 11

## *Sea Sisters*

As Tiny and Father left our orbit, new friends took their place: sisters named Lan and Linh. Their family did not use nicknames, and since both knew how to read and write—a big accomplishment for Vietnamese girls anywhere—we didn't rename them. It was a matter of respect.

They came to Hong Kong as we did, by sea, but from the ancient city of Hue, Vietnam's Capital of Kings. I assumed this meant Lan and Linh were royalty, too, but they said most of their family's wealth had been taken by the new regime. For them, the Odyssey at sea had been a great leveler. They were now as poor as the rest of us, with prospects just as uncertain.

Still, with more education between them than my whole family put together, they were smart, good-humored, and inventive—just what Dimples and I needed to refresh our wilting spirits. Their family lived in Father's camp where the bigger shelters had ladders going up to the roof. We scooped out a hole under the fence that divided their camp from ours and, following their lead, climbed a ladder at twilight to spy on camp lovers as they watched the sunset. We giggled and made up our own dialog for them, or just made animal noises and ducked down when they turned to look. When one was taking a photo, we'd hustle to get in the background. We weren't naughty, just mischievous. It felt good to have fun again.

On one of these occasions, a young man shook his fist at us and said, "If you don't stop bothering us, I'll bag you like a frog!" I had no idea what that meant until Lan explained it.

"Frog-catching is big business," she said, "didn't you know? Lots of people go out in the evening when the frogs start croaking, put them in sacks or jars then sell them at the wet market—right next to the snakes and turtles."

"Let's go frog-catching right now!" Dimples was halfway down the ladder.

"Yeah," I was right behind her. "We can sure use the money."

"Wait," Lan said, "Where's your stuff? Do you know what to bring? What to wear? This isn't like going downtown!"

She was right. We agreed to change clothes and get our equipment and meet at the sliding gate when the guards turned on the lights.

At the appointed time, when the sky glowed red and the perimeter lights switched on, Dimples and I arrived at the gate in nice dresses with two big plastic bags freshly liberated from the trash cans near Father's compound. When Lan and Linh showed up, our mouths dropped open. In place of their pretty play-clothes, they wore the dirtiest rags they could find—torn t-shirts and old shorts. They also had the sense to bring a flashlight.

"You guys going to a party?" Lan asked.

"We're frog-hunting, like you," I answered, feeling dumber than ever.

"You'll be sorry," Linh said. "We'll spend half the night in the swamp, most of it in the mud. Usually we just find garbage. You didn't even bring a flashlight! Hope you don't mind snakes."

It was too late to turn back now, and if we waited too long all the frogs near the road would be taken. We showed our passes to the guard who took one look at us, shook his head and let us through.

An hour later, our arms and legs were covered with crap—literally—since rural Chinese heeded the call of nature just by stepping off the road. Worse, we had nothing to show for our labor.

"I quit," I said, trying not to sound like a quitter. "I think you guys made it up."

"No, really" Linh said. "Frogs are all around here. We just have to look in the right spots. See? There's one over there!"

She shined the flashlight onto a circle of reeds where a bumpy lump rested half-out of the water. Lan followed her sister's beam, grabbed the lump and pulled it up.

"See? Frog!" The half-eaten carcass stared back with lifeless eyes. Its tiny arms led to an exposed backbone without legs.

"Okay, I'm leaving," Dimples dumped her bag. Since Linh had the only flashlight, she quit the hunt and lit a path back to the road so Dimples wouldn't break her neck. Lan and I splashed after them.

When we got home, Dimples and I sneaked back Father's room where we'd been staying to be close to our new friends. Thankfully, Father and Tiny were snoring. We dumped our wet clothes and put on our pajamas, certain we'd come up with a plausible story for our ruined dresses by the time the sun came up.

After the failed frog hunt, the four of us decided to spend more time in town. The new girls were adventurous but inexperienced, so Dimples and I put the training we'd received from Tiny to good use, if not always to good credit.

Dimples, for example, had developed a taste for alcohol This went back to our days in An Hai when she sampled the brandy and vodka our guardians left on our ancestral shrine. Father cured her of that simply by saying that their ghosts would haunt anyone who stole their booze. Tiny introduced us to beer, which in Hong Kong was easy to get with no dead ancestors attached. Like Lan and Linh, Dimples knocked back one can every time we went to town. Amazingly, none of them got drunk. Dimples said it made her feel ngao, like a leaf in the wind, and that's when she knew she'd had enough. Linh and Lan seemed unfazed, although they often split a can and made it last all night. For me, drinking beer was like drinking pee. I hated the acrid smell, the yellow color and the acid taste; and the fumes from a just-opened can made me dizzy. I was much better with cigarettes, having learned to inhale on my Granduncle's knee as he showed me how roll-your-own and light it. Still, the other girls didn't smoke and I didn't like it well enough to invest in a whole pack—I had better uses for Father's Hong Kong dollars. This dispute about high living, it turned out, sparked the first falling-out between Dimples and me as sisters.

"You guys are boring," Dimples announced one evening as we nursed our beers in a downtown park. "Father knows how to party—Captain Six told me about it. He said Father has a girlfriend and they go to all kinds of places."

"That's not true," I said. "Father has a wife at home—or somewhere. He's saving his money to bring her here, or take her to America. Don't believe what the Captain tells you. Sometimes he likes to joke."

"This is no joke. I saw what Father did to Tiny. I know you helped him hide it. Tiny got beat-up and went to the hospital just to get me that pretty purse. He wants me to have a good time and now Father makes him live like a monk. If Father won't take me out with his girlfriend, I'll tell him I'm going to steal that pink purse again and call the police. I'll tell them Tiny did it. Father's afraid they'll lock him away, so he'll do whatever I say!"

I'd never heard my little sister talk like that and as she stormed away, Linh got up to stop her but I said, "No, let her go. She's just a baby. A big baby. And so what if Father has a girlfriend? Lots of camp men do. Maybe your father has one, too!"

Now I was talking in a way I'd never heard. What was the beer doing to us? What was this place doing to us?

I thought Lan and Linh would be insulted, coming from an old and respected family, but they just laughed and chugged their beer. The world had turned upside down. Was I the only one to see it?

The next few days were hell. Dimples pouted and tried to manipulate Father any way she could: with tears, with threats, with false accusations about me (well, maybe not all of them false), even saying what a bad influence our new pals had been on us, but nothing convinced him to take her on dates with his girlfriend, or even to admit he had one. Although she was careful to avoid his wrath, Dimples hinted that he was being too strict with Tiny, but maybe she still had that pink purse in mind. Anyway, the more she pouted or raved or pushed me away, the quieter Father got, as if retreating into a cave. That left me feeling more alone than ever. Was this why I stole aboard fishing boat Number 6 and braved the storms at sea? Was this the better life Mama had promised us?

The only solution was to avoid my relatives altogether, even Captain Six who had never done me any wrong and was always a source of good advice. I took camp meals with Lan and Linh's family and we made even longer trips to town, sometimes staying way past curfew and sleeping in a park or an alley then walking through the gate in the morning with the first wave of returning shoppers. The guards didn't care. Father didn't care. Tiny and Dimples didn't care and even worse, I didn't care—until one night when I had a fight with Lan and Linh.

I don't remember what it was about. We were downtown drinking and they wanted to go somewhere I didn't, so after arguing a minute I just flipped them off and went back to camp. I didn't want to deal with Father, so I went back to my old bed in the Captain's room. When I got there, Dimples was crying softly in her usual place on the floor. I stepped over her and sat on the edge of the lower bunk. The Captain was above me, smoking a cigar.

"Why is Dimples back so soon?" I asked him. "I thought she was going to town with Father."

"You mean, why is she crying?" Captain Six asked. As usual, the Captain had read my mind. "Your father finally took Dimples along on an outing with your Uncle Six and me. As we walked along the highway, your uncle and father started to argue. He accused your father of training a bad wife, which is why he needed a girlfriend. Your mother was supposed to get your Uncle Six's children out of Vietnam first, before her own, who are younger and have lower priority. That's how things are done. So your uncle blamed your father for failing the family. This made your Father mad, so he picked up Dimples and asked your uncle if he wanted him to throw her into traffic to even the score."

"That can't be!" I gasped. "Father would never do that—" then I thought of the way he had beaten Tiny and said, "Uncle Six would never allow it!"

"Your uncle just egged him on. Said he was too big a coward to go through with his threat, but I'm sure he didn't mean it. Your uncle was just angry. Of course, Buddha forbids a younger brother from striking an elder, so all your father could do was drop Dimples on the sidewalk and wave his fists. That's when I picked her up and ran back to camp."

"Was Father drunk?" I asked.

"They'd both been drinking, but that's not the point. Grown men do what they have to do. Little Dimples is the one I'm worried about."

The Captain lay back on his bunk and puffed a smoke ring from his cigar, which was fine because I was totally speechless. Although I was ashamed to say it, or even think it, I felt relieved. Now Dimples was just like me: no father, no uncle, no brother, no big sister to look after her. We were back where we started, two pipsqueaks in a leaky old boat with no life raft. We could only depend on each other.

Dimples and I began to hang out again, but things had changed between us. Where I used to decide where we went and what we'd do, Dimples now made plans of her own.

"We've got to stop Father from wrecking the family," she said as we sipped sodas on the roof of Father's shelter—the same place where we used to play with Lan and Linh. "He's going to leave Mama and marry his girlfriend. He may even stay with her in Hong Kong. So much for America."

"What can we do about it?" I asked.

"We can kill her," Dimples drained her can noisily. "We can stab her in her sleep."

Whoa! Father's Kung-Fu fighting-fisherman's blood ran stronger in Dimples' veins than I realized! At first I thought she was kidding.

"What about Father?" I asked. "He has to show you where she lives, and when they're together, they're bound to sleep in the same bed, like Mama and Father did at home."

"Then we'll kill him, too," Dimples crushed her can in the middle.

"Well," I cleared my throat like a sensible big-sister, "I don't think it will come to that. Father doesn't want to dishonor his ancestors. He wants to go to America. Just look at all the trouble he went to cover Tiny and that pink purse. We just need to leave him alone until we get permission to go. Like the captain always says, everything will be fine."

I almost believed it myself.

# 12

## *Sea Birds*

Once a captain, always a captain. I guess the commander of fishing boat Number 6 didn't feel his duty was done until we'd reached our final destination: America. Of course, he didn't want a mutiny on his hands, so he decided to nip our disaffection in the bud.

Out of the blue, he invited as many of his previous passengers as he could find to a private dinner in our sleeping area. This was unusual, since Captain Six mostly kept to himself or hung out with the older refugees; or cultivated good relations with officials to make sure our paperwork kept moving. One way or another, the Captain was always on duty.

Dimples and I were flattered by the invitation and accepted mostly because we couldn't find a polite way to say no. Father was still a virtual stranger more interested in his mistress than in us, though for self-protection we maintained our roles as dutiful daughters, making sure we didn't anger or embarrass him. Tiny spent more time away from camp—not downtown causing mischief, but visiting the Sisters at the hospital who had interested him in Christ. The Buddhism we knew had lots of rituals but not much mystery at its core—at least for us kids. We accepted all we were told and trusted magic to run the Universe. Catholics on the other hand, had an explanation for everything and for a young teenager trapped by conflicting forces—family, police, camp guards, and peers—the idea of divine forgiveness by a loving savior was, for him, a life saver. He visited their church often, went to Mass, prayed in their chapel, and it seemed to help him bear his cross. He even got Dimples and me to attend Mass one Sunday on the promise of free treats: the nuns often gave poor families food and clothing at the end of a service—but not on the day we went. Dimples and I felt cheated but Tiny told us to return next week. We liked the church's candles and costumes but had no idea what was going on. So after asking Jesus's forgiveness, we said amen to future visits. Amazingly, Tiny said he understood and accepted our decision like a saint.

Also present at the Captain's dinner was Uncle Six, a man neither of us much trusted. Dimples couldn't understand why he failed to protect her on that terrible night by the highway. As for me, I always had the feeling Uncle Six was working some angle, playing some game, though I couldn't say what. As long as I didn't have to depend on him for anything, though, I could keep my distance and it wouldn't matter.

It turned out that our little party was the first of several the Captain had planned. That first night, we sat in a circle with our food trays and ate politely, talking inoffensively about this and that: the events of the day (which were few) and the weather. Nobody said anything about Chinese girlfriends or throwing people into traffic or if anybody had any interesting police stories to share. That alone—plus the fresh apples the Captain had somehow wrangled for desert—made the evening actually pleasant. When he invited everyone again a few days later, Dimples and I looked forward to it.

When it became obvious at these gatherings that nobody was going to tear off anyone's head, we began to talk about more important things, like how the camp police were handling the major and minor riots; which people finally got their golden pass to America and which families seemed forever trapped in limbo; we even told some jokes. While all this went on, Captain Six said less and less, but just rested on his elbows, smiling, until the dinner was over then lit his cigar. Despite ourselves, and under the Ccaptain's thoughtful tutelage, we were learning how to be a family again. It turned out we were also becoming something more.

Most men visited the camp bulletin board at least once a day, usually toward the evening when the latest news was posted. Most important were the lists of families and individuals who had been sponsored for immigration. America was everyone's first choice, but any former Southern ally like Australia, New Zealand, Canada, even France was fine too—anything that got us out of camp. A big reason America was favored is that its culture was most familiar. U.S. soldiers and civilians filled the South for decades leaving a legacy of buildings, utilities, cars, consumer goods—all the things that Northern officials warned us were signs of evil capitalism—though that didn't stop the new regime from confiscating and using them. Most important, many families had relatives in America. These weren't just boat people like us, though our numbers mounted daily, but Vietnamese resettled before the war ended in 1975 as dependents of U.S. citizens. Father was usually first to check new postings, and each day left disappointed. Every day his name did not appear seemed to slice away part of his spirit.

But not today.

Early in September, Father's and Tiny's name appeared on a list of Vietnamese with sponsors in San Francisco—an immigrant-friendly community well-known around the camps. It was second only to "Little Saigon" in Los Angeles and the Vietnamese fisherman's enclave in Houston—a place whose weather most closely resembled An Hai's—as the destination of choice in America. Father was ecstatic.

"This is it! We have a date!" Father said excitedly as he came late to the Captain's dinner party. "September 24, 1979," he beamed, "that's the golden day!"

"What about Dimples and me?" I asked.

Father's grin faded. He didn't say it, but it was obvious. Our names were not on the list. According to British records, we were officially the Captain's children and their policy was to keep families together.

Father didn't bother to sit down. Instead, he went straight to the guard shack by the gate where most of the custodians worked or took their breaks. Dimples and I ran after him. We arrived in time to hear him tell a supervisor, "But they are my daughters! I won't leave without my daughters!"

The official opened a file, read silently then said, "You have a nephew in San Francisco, right? His name is Nhanh?"

Good old Cousin Nhanh! He'd made it first and didn't forget us—at least not Tiny and Father. He must've sponsored Father and Tiny before we made it to camp. Still, the sponsorship letter was a beacon of hope in the fog.

"Yes, yes," Father said, "Nhanh is my brother's son. He's our sponsor in America."

"Well," the supervisor wrinkled his brow, "he remembered you and your son. But the application says nothing about daughters."

"Then I'll send a telegram. I'll get authorization from the source!" Father stormed from the little office, a man on a mission—a big switch for him because he usually let officials have the last word. Now he was a lion—so much so, in fact, I began to worry that he might flip-out and punch somebody if he didn't get his way. He flashed his ID badge and disappeared beyond the gate, headed for the downtown telegraph office—whatever that was. We didn't have our badges with us and wouldn't know where to find him if we did, so Dimples and I just parked ourselves by the entrance and waited for him to return. A couple of hours later, he did.

"What are you girls doing here?" Father asked. "Where's Tiny?"

"Probably in his bunk. He missed dinner with the Captain. Maybe he already heard the news."

Father frowned and grumbled—never a good sign. "You girls go back to the Captain's shelter. We'll get action when Nhanh reads my telegram. For now, you're still on the rolls as the Captain's daughters. When word comes from Nhanh, the supervisor will go there to tell you. So scoot. I'll look for Tiny."

Dimples and I spent the night on an emotional roller coaster. One minute we were deliriously happy—the family had a sponsor, someone the authorities would listen to. The next minute we were down in the dumps: paper daughters of a fictitious father listed under two phony names. I figured that if it took this long for cousin Nhanh to spring Father and Tiny, who had been in the camps much longer, it might take them years to get around to us. Dimples said that maybe Jesus liked Tiny best because he went to church and held it against us because we didn't. The Captain said little except he was sorry if the adoption papers were holding us up. At the time, he said, they were the only thing that kept us sisters together and out of an orphanage. "If you got lost in that system," he said "no one would ever find you." That shut us up, but we still sent a few silent prayers to Buddha, the Goddess of Mecy, and Jesus. At least it gave us something to do while we waited and—lo and behold—it got results.

The next afternoon as we gathered for our now-traditional Captain's meal, Father arrived with a small, yellow paper. Apparently that's what a telegram looked like. "You can relax!" he said with a big, golden grin. "This is from Nhanh. Everyone's going to America!"

Well, not everyone. The list now included those members of Father's family that had made it to Hong Kong. The fate of Mama and Pudgy, Brat and Fly Swat was still a mystery. Had they left Vietnam? Had the police re-arrested Mama after Dimples and I disappeared? Were our sister and brothers now burdening relatives in An Hai, or even worse—roaming the streets of Da Nang? We couldn't know and it hurt too much to guess, so we didn't. Instead, we dug into the Captain's dinner and talked about America.

"You know, Americans eat beef and potatoes," Father said. "They have no fish or rice. I heard that from a guy who gets letters from abroad. They eat only hamburgers and fried potatoes and Cokes and candy. So eat all the fish and rice you can until we get on the airplane—ten times a day if we have to. I want to take the memory of our traditional food with us."

Actually, a steady diet of soda and candy and barbeque beef—a treat even for Vietnamese—didn't sound so bad but I kept my mouth shut. Father was happy and it was lovely, for a change, to see those gold teeth through a smile.

On September 23rd, the day before our departure, we packed a few belongings in a tote bag and gave everything else to our campmates. Our gifts consisted mostly of clothes, but Father did donate the transistor radio he'd saved to buy with his small salary. At first, Dimples wouldn't go along with it. It's hard for kids to give away anything, especially when they start with so little, and the nun's lessons about the virtue of charity hadn't yet sunk in, but my example and Father's logic saved the day.

"We'll get plenty of free things in America," he said. "Their country is even richer than Hong Kong and their people are more generous than the Chinese. You'll see. I'll bet your cousin Nhanh lives like a king!"

The next morning—our last in the camp—we ate fish and rice (naturally) with the Captain and Hung, made a joyous, tearful goodbye to the camp friends who came to see us off, then gathered with the other selected families by the gate to await the airport bus. It would be a long trip to America, but at last we were taking the first step.

Hong Kong International was a land-fill airport jutting out from the diamond city. Crossing the causeway, I felt like we were leaving not just the glass towers but a long and miserable nightmare behind forever.

A camp-translator escorted us to the ticket counter and stood by while family after family presented their credentials. When it was our turn, the ticket lady looked perturbed.

"The manifest lists you and your son," she said to Father through the interpreter, "but we have no record of your daughters. Are you sure they're on the same flight?"

Father had no idea what she meant and I saw the frustration build in his face. He fished the telegrams out of his tote, along with the camp's revised sponsor list, and slapped them on the counter. "There!" he said through the translator, "there's our paperwork. My daughters were added after the first list came out. Here, read the telegram. They have the same sponsor as us. It's my nephew in San Francisco. Look. It's all there."

The ticket lady called her supervisor, a Chinese man busy with other howling customers down the counter. He didn't look sympathetic and I felt the volcano rising. Another airline man stepped over.

"What's going on?" Father asked the translator. "What are they saying? I'm not leaving without my daughters!"

"They say it's not the airline's problem. They only do what the British tell them and since they only saw the first list, those are the people with tickets. Apparently nobody gave them the new one."

"But they have the new one now!" Father said.

"That came from you, not the officials. Somebody should've told the airline. It's not official until it's been stamped and signed and—"

"Then get somebody to stamp and sign it!" Father bellowed. "Get somebody on the phone. Call somebody in authority. Call America!"

The passengers behind us were getting impatient, which only increased Father's frustration and embarrassment. That was not a good sign.

"Okay, you kids wait over there," the camp translator pointed to a big lounge area. "Your father and I will sort things out. Don't worry. You'll get on the airplane. Everything will be fine."

We'd heard that before. The odd thing was, that's how it usually turned out—but Father was very impatient. He'd had it with all the red tape and demanded to speak with a senior official. I could still hear them arguing as Tiny escorted us to a bench. The lounge was filled with all types of people—men in turbans and women in long silk dresses, men in business suits and flight crews in sharp uniforms. Announcements we couldn't understand echoed over the loudspeaker and a big wall sign flashed letters and numbers we couldn't read. Strange little rooms with no windows or back doors—elevators Tiny called them—dinged and people got in, disappeared, then came out as someone else. Glass doors opened and closed onto the street as bag-laden people arrived and went. Policemen strolled by, checking us out, as if sizing us up for a bus ride back to camp.

"Now you guys behave yourselves," Tiny said like a stern nun. "Don't touch anything. If you break something, they'll make us pay for it."

Dimples and I sat on adjoining chairs and watched Father wheel-and-deal from a distance. I was just glad I didn't hear what was going on. Officials came and went, some in jackets and ties, some in shirt sleeves. With so many people making such a big fuss over two little girls, it was a wonder any airliner got off the ground!

Tiny knew how to tell time and said that according to one big clock on the wall, there was only an hour left until our flight. He said passengers would be boarding soon and if Father didn't wrap things up, we'd be waving goodbye to him from the boarding gate. Father might not leave without his daughters, but I got the feeling it would not stop Tiny. It turned out, we needn't have worried.

Father came over to our bench with a new stack of papers, duly signed and stamped, and said through his gold teeth: "Come on. Let's go to America!"

We jumped up joyfully with our tote bag.

"Only thing is," he said, "they need your pictures. Come back to the counter and an airline girl will take some hurry-up photos. Come on. Quick, quick, quick!"

I had no idea how a camera could take and show a photo in a minute, but it did. In fact, it took several for each of us and Father placed them among the papers then hustled us off toward the boarding gate where we bumped into another line.

From there, we shuffled like prisoners to a clanky metal ramp and through spooky door that looked like a bank vault. A pretty lady in a blue uniform and scarf welcomed me to—somewhere—and pointed our family down the aisle. We crab-stepped past old ladies and children and impatient white and Chinese men putting bags in the overhead bins and finally found the row of seats that matched the numbers on our card. It was pure bedlam and nobody could decide which seat was theirs until a different pretty lady told each of us in fractured Vietnamese, "you here, you there, you here, you on the end" so that's where we wound up.

Our row was in the middle of the plane, but at least we were together. I was immediately jealous of the kids, less well-behaved than me and Dimples, who got to sit next to a window and press their nose against the glass. It was like they had the whole world in their lap.

"Here, put on your seat belts," Father said, after the flight attendant showed him how. Gradually, the people in the long, long cabin settled down and my head felt stuffy when the big door shut and the overhead lights blinked and a man's voice came over the intercom like the loudspeakers in a camp and said something in several languages, none of which I understood. The air outside began to roar and the cabin jerked backward the way our stilt-room felt in a monsoon but nobody seemed to notice. From the peeks I stole through the distant windows, I saw the terminal building move backward, then stop, then slowly move away. The flight attendants passed up and down the aisles, double-checking our seat belts. She smiled at us, so we apparently passed inspection.

"Okay, we're going to take off," Father said from the seat next to mine. It was only then, I think, I realized I would soon be floating through the air the way I did in my dreams with Father Dragon. It was one of many scary and exhilarating moments I'd already seen on my long voyage to America. I couldn't wait for more.

The takeoff felt like a bad night on boat Number 6. The wings began to whine and I was pressed against my seat and Dimples squeezed my hand so hard that I couldn't feel my fingers. The floor beneath me clumped then whole cabin tilted then straightened then tilted again, making me feel dizzy on top of scared. My ears popped and so did Dimples.' That's when she broke her death-grip on my hand in order to grab the sides of her head. The flight attendant appeared and offered each of us a stick of gum. Why anyone would distribute treats at a time like this was beyond me, but if the stewardess wasn't afraid, then I guessed we shouldn't be either, so each of us took a piece.

"Chew these," she said with the pretty smile. "It will make your ears feel better."

We did, and it did. The cabin leveled again, though it felt like we were pointed at the moon, and aside from the howling wind outside and the little vents blowing cold air high above our seats, the world was returning to normal. Still, riding the Dragon's back was nothing like it had been in my dreams.

The flight proceeded comfortably despite occasional bumps in the sky. The sun sank behind us and the window-people pulled down their shades, spoiling what little view we center-aislers stole from either side.

"They will start the feature film shortly," the stewardess who spoke Vietnamese said. She was kept very busy in our part of the plane. "If you want to use the bathroom, now would be a good time." She gave each of us a set of Y-shaped tubes with earmuffs on one end and what looked like a hose nozzle on the other. I had no idea what these were for and decided to worry about them later.

I asked Father where the bathrooms were and he pointed down the aisle several rows behind us where a line had already formed. The little doors looked like the ones on the port-a-potties adults used in the warehouse camp yuck! Nobody cleaned up after themselves so they always looked and smelled like crap. I vowed to hold my pee until we landed in San Francisco—how much longer could that be? I changed my mind when I found out.

The business at hand, though, was to get my ear things to work, so I watched the other passengers. One seasoned traveler across the aisle put the earmuffs on and plugged the hose into her armrest. I copied her and got a blast of American music so I jerked it out and leaned over Dimples toward Tiny and asked for advice. He shook his head disdainfully and showed me the little wheel that controlled the volume and another little wheel that set the channel, like tuning Father's radio. I couldn't decide which music to stick with, so I switched through them all again and again. Soon the attendant pulled down a little screen on a bulkhead many rows in front of us and except for a couple of glowing signs above the doorways and little blinky lights that went on and off over various seats, the entire cabin went dark. A second later the blank channel I'd flipped through came alive and colored pictures appeared on the screen. I helped Dimples rig her gear and her sound came on just as the open credits appeared. "Superman!" said someone in the row behind me, and from the look of the people who first filled the screen, it was a window on an American village.

Needless to say, although I couldn't understand a word, I fell in love with Superman. He was super strong and super handsome with a super smile that melted my heart. I couldn't understand, though, why he spoiled his good looks with glasses he didn't need and covered up his colorful suit—more spectacular than the Lion Dancers' costumes in our village—just to impress his mousy girlfriend. The next movie was a "western," but these Americans were grimy and rude and wore dirty brown clothes. It was boring except for the shooting which made me jump. I'd heard plenty of that when I was a little kid in our bunker and I still remembered that terrible shot while I was hiding on the captain's boat. Such noises blasting again in the big bouncing airliner in the middle of the night over the middle of the ocean was not my idea of entertainment. I wanted to see Superman again so I could feel warm and secure.

"Hey, come on!" Tiny whispered, reading my mind. "They're playing Superman in the front of the plane." We yanked the hose out of our armrests and still wearing the headsets moved up the sloping aisle until a less-nice stewardess stopped us at a curtain. She made it plain by her expression and wagging finger that we were not allowed in this special area. What made it special? I peeked around the curtain and saw lots of blond-haired women and men in nice shirts all sitting in extra wide seats with fancy drinks on their tray tables. All had round eyes and skin lighter than any Asian.

"Americans," Tiny whispered as the flight attendant gently turned us around. I wasn't sure I could do much about my skin color, but I was determined to one day ride in those fancy seats. One day, I too would be an American.

Hours later, the sun rose off the airliner's nose. It must've looked spectacular from where the pilot sat, but from our seats in the middle row way in the back, with most of the window shades closed, all I saw were rosy fingers spread out on the horizon over the pitch-black water below. People began to stir. Lines formed again at the bathrooms. The potties weren't so bad—the flight attendants obviously tried to keep them as nice and fresh as their own uniforms, but after so long a flight, even those were beginning to look tired.

I was glad when Father, waking up in his usual gruff way, glanced at his watch and said the flight would be over soon.

Hot towels, juice, toast and fresh fruit—a big improvement over the tasteless American food we were served before the film—I might survive in America after all, even without Father's fish and rice! Most of the window shades were up now and the day was bright outside. Another announcement on the PA and people began to chew gum again, so Dimples and I took another stick. The noise outside dropped lower, as did the plane, little by little, until some fluffy clouds flashed by and I could see, even from my middle seat, the face of the ocean and a sliver of brown land. My ears popped again—worse than before. I told myself it was just Father Dragon telling us goodbye as we came under the wing of our new American guardian: the super man in the super red cape. I wondered if, after Father and Tiny and Dimples and I became Americans, we would look like the rich, stylish people in front of the curtain.

And if we did, would Mama still recognize us?

# 13

## *Crow's Nest*

"Safra Siko," the Vietnamese lady across the aisle explained to her kids the name of the cool, gray city outside her window as we taxied to the terminal. The airliner bumped to a stop, a little bell chimed, and the lights on the bulkhead went off. Everybody stood at the same time, even those hunched under the curved cabin, now regretting their coveted window seats. Overhead bins popped open. People hustled to get their stuff then shuffled into the aisles to wait, wait, and wait. With everyone else, we stood like cattle until the vault-door up front popped open. Still, after being cooped up for so many hours, it felt good to see, if not yet breathe, the fresh air outside.

We shuffled past the pretty ladies in uniform, lined up to say "bye-bye"—my first really useful English phrase. The air in the gangway was clean and breezy and walking down its long corridor felt like being reborn. Beyond the ramp a big room spread out with more long lines leading to more tables where more uniformed custodians—some Chinese as well as white—sat like judges examining our papers, our pictures, and us. We had no checked luggage, so we went right to the inspectors, a familiar feeling from the Hong Kong camps. A veteran line-stander, I had plenty of time to study the people of our new nation.

White people seemed familiar now with their hair of many hues, round eyes, and long (sometimes huge!) noses; but I was not prepared for so many black people, both passengers and workers (with their own startling array of skin tones), and "Latinos" who looked vaguely Vietnamese. None of these exotic specimens wore their national costumes, as we did with our white blouses and shirts, blue shorts or skirts, black pajamas or ao dais—the flowing pant-dresses that made any Vietnamese woman look like royalty. I felt like I had discovered some other kid's coloring book with all the people filled in. I had nothing to do but gawk.

When it was our turn at the tables, the bored customs man stamped our papers yet again and returned them to Father. As we moved down the rope-line toward—where?—a voice at the edge of the lobby called in Vietnamese.

"Hey! Uncle Seven!" It was Cousin Nhanh, our sponsor, our savior. He looked pretty much as I remembered him from a couple of years ago, except in place of his fisherman's work shirt he wore a sports coat and looked prosperous.

Men seldom embraced in Vietnam, regardless of the situation, so they shook hands energetically, bracing each other's forearm to show extra warmth then bowed politely. When Father waved his arm in our direction, we bowed too. Cousin Nhanh smiled and said he remembered us well. It was only now that I realized how kind America had been to him during his first year. He looked healthy—like a prize athlete next to Father, who still bore the mark of camp rations in his thin arms and of too much alcohol in the bags under his eyes. I assumed a year in America would cure him of all that.

Cousin Nhanh led us through the international terminal to a busy street where cars pulled up discharging and collecting passengers. Inside the covered garage, Nhanh led us through a maze of cars to where his old brown sedan was parked. A car like this would denote great wealth in An Hai, but here—next to the snazzy late-model cars around it—it looked like a jalopy. I now began to suspect that America may not have been as kind to Cousin Nhanh as I supposed.

It took him several tries to start he car, raising a cloud of smoke. We pulled into the swirling traffic and I asked Cousin Nhanh if the tall stone and glass buildings in the distance were where we were going to live. I was secretly dreading life in another big diamond.

"No," Nhanh said as we skirted the glittering buildings on a raised highway and entered a long silver bridge to the east. "We're going to Oakland. That's where most new arrivals settle. It's much better than the Tenderloin in San Francisco. Since '75 the City has gotten too crowded. Too many winos. Too much crime. You're going to like your new home."

Whatever this Oakland was like, it had to be better than jammed camps, clapboard shelters, or warehouses stuffed with people. Cousin Nhanh continued to sing its praises as the cars and trucks ahead of us slowed then finally stopped in a cascade of red and white tail lights that went as far as the eye could see.

"Quitting time traffic!" Cousin Nhanh shook his head. "I hate it!"

While Father and his nephew talked in the front seat about the village since Nhanh left in 1976, we three kids spoke quietly in the back.

"Who is Cousin Nhanh again?" Dimples whispered.

"He fought for the South," Tiny told her. "After the war, he went through re-education then came home. The year after that, Cousin Nhanh took his fishing boat to Hong Kong. That was three years ago. After a while some church people sponsored him and he got a job in Oakland. That's why he was able to sponsor us."

"What about Mama and Pudgy and Brat and Fly Swat?" Dimples asked.

Tiny shrugged. "I don't know. Ask Cousin Nhanh."

Eventually, we peeled off the highway into a city of smaller high-rises called Oakland. Nhanh braked at the entrance to an underground garage at 14th Street and Alice, just a few blocks from a pretty park called Lake Merritt. He made a grand gesture out his window toward an old three story apartment building on the corner.

"That's it!" he declared. "That's home!"

Father beamed, "Ah, you did very well for yourself. Only here for two years and you already own a fine building!"

"Oh no," Nhanh laughed. "I rent a unit on the second floor. Nobody has enough money to buy real estate around here. For the price of one house in the Oakland hills, you could buy the whole village of An Hai!"

"Well then, that will give us something to work for," Father seemed relieved that Nhanh's tall shadow had been reduced at least a little.

In a way, the apartment building was like our stilt houses back home, resting on a series of thin columns in the parking garage that supported the rest of the structure. I hoped they would be strong enough when the rainy season hit, but I didn't want to sound critical, so I kept my mouth shut. Cousin Nhanh led us to the building's magical elevator—a smaller version of the one we'd ridden in the Hong Kong airport. He pressed "2" and we started up.

Nhanh's unit was at the end of a dimly lit hallway. He unlocked the door and ushered us in.

"It's just two bedrooms with one bath, but we've lived in worse places. Look—I have a TV!" he pointed pridefully to the small box in the corner. "I even have a stereo so the kids can listen to music."

We all took off our shoes at the entrance and the carpet instantly massaged my feet—heaven for a usually barefoot girl who'd had them cased in leather for a day and a night. I was amazed cousin Nhanh didn't say more about this best feature of his home.

Room by room, he showed us around: a padded chair and sofa, bouncy soft beds and indoor plumbing for kitchen and bathroom that actually worked. He even had a telephone, which let you talk to people far away without shouting. Distant people, though, were not our immediate problem.

"So, how many people can live here?" Father asked. He, too, noticed the small rooms and short hallway with very few closets. It would be a tight fit for all of us.

"As many as we can squeeze in," Nhanh replied, "but some of the space is already taken. Besides me, there's Uncle Six—he arrived last week—plus my five brothers who I sponsored last year. With you four, that makes eleven, but don't worry. Once you register for public assistance, you'll be in-line to get your own place. They give priorities to families with kids."

"How about food?" Father was always practical. "How will we do all that cooking?"

"No problem," Nhanh replied. "Fast-food restaurants are cheap and there's a supermarket around the corner."

"Supermarket?"

"You know, a market like Superman. Really big—has everything you want in cans or packages or in the freezer."

Superman! Now there was a market I had to see!

"Don't worry about it," Nhanh said confidently, showing us where to put the things from our tote bag. "Everything will be fine."

***

That evening, we visited our first American supermarket: a place called Lucky—a good omen. Lighting up an entire block and with self-propelled sliding doors, it looked like a place Superman himself would shop!

Inside were even more surprises. The first was: no flies, the hallmark of every Vietnamese market. The second was: no smell. Well, that's not true, if it smelled like anything it was like Tiny's Hong Kong hospital. This was a mixed blessing. Our noses had been trained from birth to guide us to wholesome food, be it from the sea or from the earth. Here, plastic covered everything, even the pre-gutted fish, chopped pork, and chicken parts. (Yes, America had plenty of fish and rice—Father's friend was wrong about that.) Finally, nobody haggled over price. All money-talk was between machines: the ones that put price tags on what you bought and the register than rang them up. All the customer had to do was shut up and pay. I wasn't sure this was an improvement over our way of doing things, but it made the lines move faster. Father had concerns on this last point.

"Don't spend too much on us," he cautioned Nhanh, comparing the price tags on goods in the aisles. Beef, a luxury back home even in a can, particularly concerned him. He pointed to another shelf where one could buy dog or cat meat in similar cans for much less. "Those will be fine," he said.

Nhanh laughed so hard I thought he would choke. "Now you sound like refugees!" he said. "That's food for pets. Little animals don't scrounge for bugs and mice in America. Here, their owners buy them special food." If dogs and cats didn't help keep snakes and rodents out of your house, I wondered, what was the point of having them? Apparently, this was the first of many riddles I'd have to solve to become an American.

Now that I'd discovered some of the differences between my old home and my new one, I began to notice their similarities. Father still had his rules, but so did Cousin Nhanh. Father was our parent, but Nhanh was our host—and as the man whose name was on the lease, Lord of the Manor as well. We kids had a curfew, just as we had in camp, and Nhanh forbade us to go outside in our pajamas—even though those were our usual work-and-play clothes in Vietnam. We also had to wear shoes anytime we went beyond his door, and he insisted we re-tune our palates for American food, which we ate at every meal—even though most of it was so rich and fatty it made me gag, or was so tasteless it was like eating the container. He was also a stickler for cleanliness. That at least made sense. My hair had finally grown past my ears, but using a comb on a scabby scalp was torture; as was my twice-daily encounter with a toothbrush. How could something that made your gums bleed every time you used it be good for you? In Vietnam and in the camps, we cleaned our teeth with bamboo shoots and minty leaves and got by just fine.

On the other hand, Nhanh rewarded good behavior. We kids couldn't get enough TV, especially cartoons like Tom and Jerry where noise and music and the characters' silly actions told the story better than words. Best of all, anyone in a cartoon who got blown up or fell off a cliff or got shot by a gun always came back to life in the next scene—resurrected just like Jesus with no three-day waiting period. They were great. We also loved the ads, which adults ignored or used for potty breaks. We especially loved one fat man who sold cars—acres and acres of cars and trucks at prices no one could beat. Gradually, we came to appreciate where Americans got their sense of invincibility and lust for more and more stuff.

In the end, despite his rules and taste for Big Macs, Cousin Nhanh was not only our savior—the man who got us out of the madhouse of Hong Kong—but our guide to our new homeland. He had shown us the face of an America we could never have imagined and, amazingly, it looked a lot like us.

# 14

## *Landlocked*

A month or two after arriving, we received our first government aid. It was something called a food voucher, so we no longer depended on Nhanh for our daily bread—or Big Mac. Now all we needed was housing. It turned out Nhanh knew several landlords, most of them Chinese, including one that allowed us to settle into a much bigger two-bedroom unit on Nineteenth Street, about a quarter mile away but still within easy walking distance of Lake Merritt and our now-familiar supermarket.

Nhanh also stressed that part of being an American was becoming educated—not just in the ways of fishing and farming and basket making, but with the kind of knowledge that comes from books. I was anxious to give it a shot, though Dimples was less enthusiastic. She knew school would cost her a lot of Tom-and-Jerry time, but she was lonesome and longed for friends. Tiny was cautious. He was unsure about being thrown-in with older kids who didn't speak his language. To him, "Cleveland Elementary School," where we finally registered, looked more like place for prisoners than scholars, but he had no choice so he put his trust in Jesus, hoping the classrooms, like so many in Vietnam, would be filled with nuns. They weren't.

In the office of the registrar, where Father and cousin Nhanh completed the enrollment papers, we learned there would be another big change in our life: We would have to use new names.

Cousin Nhanh turned to us first. "You know, you can't use your family nicknames when you start your classes. You must all go by your real names, which are now your official American names. Tiny, what's your real name?"

"Xi?" Tiny was fairly certain of that.

"Twiggy?"

"Hiep," I answered. "It means togetherness." I felt smarter already.

"Okay," Nhanh turned to Dimples, "how about you?"

Dimples dug in her heels and clammed up. Here was where Father's Kung-Fu warrior-fisherman blood again came to the surface—not the best way to start our new adventure.

"Hoa," I volunteered. "Her name is Hoa. It means peace."

"Okay," Cousin Nhanh got down to her eye level. "Hoa, can you remember that? Peace is very important, which means you are very important. You want people in school to like you, right?"

"School is where people beat you up," Tiny said unhelpfully.

Dimples cut her eyes at him then back to me. Since I was speaking for her, I guess she expected a rebuttal.

"Look," I said, "in school, we'll learn to read like rich kids. What's wrong with that? Everyone's rich in America. Come on—Hoa—get with the program!"

Eventually, she did and the registrar took us to the Principal—a soft-spoken, gray-haired man who escorted us to a dirt playground with a teeter-totter, swings, kid-powered merry-go-round, slide and monkey bars. If school contained any fun, I thought, it would probably start here.

"Where are all the kids who will be my friends?" Dimples asked.

Cousin Nhanh translated for the Principal, who answered, "They're all in class now, but you'll join them shortly. Come on, I'll show you all the rest of the school."

After a while poking into "Learning Centers" and "Auditoriums" and a "Cafeteria" that smelled like barf, Tiny asked: "So, when do we get our first beating?"

Cousin Nhanh didn't translate that, but answered in Vietnamese. "In American schools, teachers never strike the students. It is forbidden. If a kid gets too rowdy, they just call his parents."

We kids took that as good news, since we'd gotten very skilled at both appeasing the police and avoiding Father's anger. I didn't know what scrapes Tiny got into in Hong Kong, but Dimples and I and our crew had never run into a problem we couldn't talk our way out of.

Our first stop after the playground was Mrs. Wong's kindergarten class, where the lady Principal introduced "Hoa" who clung desperately to my leg. Mrs. Wong was Chinese, so at least she looked like us and her voice was calm and soothing. She produced a cookie for Hoa which brought out her dimpled smile and a deal was struck. While Mrs. Wong introduced her to the other kids, the rest of us slipped out and went down the linoleum corridor to Mr. Richmond and Tiny's first dose of sixth grade.

"Xi" was not as lucky. Mr. Richmond was very, very black—a good head taller than Cousin Nhanh, who was tall for a Vietnamese—and looked like he weighed more than his whole class put together. He wore a serious gray suit with a serious expression under slicked-back, greasy black hair. He dispensed no cookies and acknowledged my brother only by pointing to an empty desk, which Tiny promptly took, then went back to his lesson on the blackboard. I was glad to be back in the hall.

"Now for Miss Hiep," the Principal said with a smile. "Second grade, isn't it? That would be Miss Lincoln." I could hardly imagine what was in store for me, and realized with each step how my misadventures in Hong Kong had ill-prepared me for life among regular kids. Where was my crew to help me out and back me up?

Fortunately, fate smiled on me that day: they were saving the best for last. Miss Lincoln was a beautiful, light-skinned blonde: as tall as Mr. Richmond but with a movie star's charisma. She was very friendly and chatty, telling her class to go back to their assignment (which had something to do with colored paper and scissors and actually looked like fun) while she chatted first with the lady Principal then to me and Father while cousin Nhanh's translation tried its best to keep up. At one point, Nhanh paused and shook his head—in disbelief or embarrassment or something—then he replied and Miss Lincoln's smile faded.

"What did she say?" I asked Cousin Nhanh, really concerned that he was blowing my good first impression.

"She said you should hug your father and kiss him goodbye so that you can get started in class."

Father and I both laughed.

"Tell her that's okay," Father said. "Tell her that's not our custom. We don't show affection in public. End of story."

"I did," Nhanh said, still uneasy. Apparently, becoming an American meant more than developing a taste for fatty foods and learning to change channels.

Fortunately, the same custom that caused our problem provided a solution. I put my feet together and gave Father a very deep and honorable bow. I then turned to Cousin Nhanh and did the same, then repeated the gesture to the lady Principal. They obviously thought that was cute, returned my bow with a polite nod then filed from the room. When they were gone, Miss Lincoln's face brightened again. She said something I didn't understand then escorted me to the head of the class—all seated on the floor in little work groups. I think she told them my name, although she spoke too fast to be sure and Hiep was not exactly a word I was used to hearing. Still, I knew my mission: to win them over, to stay out of trouble, to organize a small crew when the time was right, and maybe even learn something while I was there. It was a tall order, but I felt up to it. I had faced worse situations before. As Captain Six often said, everything will be fine.

The first lesson I learned at Cleveland School was how to act. Not how to behave, but literally how to pretend I was someone else. For example, I saw right away that being Asian was no big deal—several other kids in class and many more in the school were Chinese and they got along fine. In fact, the Asian kids did better, and were expected to do better, at their studies than most other children because the teachers thought their families helped and encouraged them at home. Well, maybe. Cousin Nhanh was more into the discipline and ritual of "going to school" than in scholarship and knowledge; and Father, who was now at home all the time, thought school was wasted on girls. My concerns were less lofty, but I lived them every day and that's where acting was handy.

I had to act like I understood Miss Lincoln, although I understood nothing she said. This was not a big challenge. All I had to do, really, was copy the other kids and mirror their expressions and I was always a good mimic. If I put on an enthusiastic face, or looked thoughtful when the teacher asked a question, I got credit for being smart without ever getting a right answer. I was already pretty good at acting innocent or worldly. Now I was learning to act smart.

Mainly, though, I had to act like I was not from a peasant fisherman's village. Since nobody understood me anyway, nobody detected my rustic An Hai dialect, but other habits die hard. I was still getting used to western toilets and knew enough to follow the girls to the bathroom during recess and when we went to lunch. The problem was, I was still having issues with American food and sometimes had to go when others didn't, and had no way of communicating this to Miss Lincoln. I got pretty good at holding things in until one day I just got up and ran out of class. I heard Miss Lincoln call my name but the bathroom was calling louder. Looking after me down the hall, she saw where I was going, smiled, and signaled me to go ahead. After that, I only had to raise my hand and point to the door and she knew what was happening, assigning a different girl from the class to accompany me each time. This turned out to be a pretty good deal for everyone. I got a break whenever I wanted and could get another girl out of class as well—just by raising my hand. Pretty soon I made the acquaintance, if the not the friendship, of every girl in the class. I had the beginning of a crew.

My acting skills came in handy at home as well. Although I looked forward to school every day, Father had his own curriculum: taken straight from an Army training manual. First, we had to go directly home after school: no dilly-dallying on the playground, no visiting friends' houses, no stopping for sodas at a store. Second, once we got home, we had to finish our chores immediately—a routine as inflexible as the chores themselves. Tiny did all the cooking (an honorable task for Vietnamese men—neighborhood eateries and food carts were common in our Homeland, and Asian chefs got jobs easily in American restaurants); I did the heavy cleaning (laundry, bathroom, dinner dishes—pots-and-pans and the like) while Dimples set and cleared the table and did a little dusting. Everyone, of course, snapped to attention when our "top sergeant" called for something, like a beer or his cigarettes or to tend the makeshift family shrine. I acted like this was fine and normal, although the more Tiny and I got to know the other kids at school, we discovered that it was not. To compensate, I spent more time inside my head: resurrecting my old invisible playmate, Mister Dragon, with whom I'd talk for hours, convincing Father once again that I was flakey and inattentive to my chores. Between the colorful new world outside and the dismal routine of the apartment, he probably was right.

By the end of our first month in school, we had our first American holiday. It was about time, we thought, since in Vietnam we had all kinds of Buddhist and Catholic holidays, as well as special days devoted to remembering family ancestors or celebrating political events. Here, Americans seemed to sweep their holidays together into seasonal groups, making sure there were plenty of work days in between. I guess that's good when your national goal is to make more money to buy more things, but even the hardest worker deserves a break—especially the hardest worker.

This particular break was known as Halloween. I had no idea what it was about, but judging from the paper ghosts and skeletons and jack-o-lanterns we made in class, and the monster masks people (even some adults!) wore in stores and in the streets, it had something to do with dead people, which we Asians knew plenty about. On the last day of October, Cousin Nhanh (whom we had not seen for a couple of weeks) met us at the front door.

"Okay, kids," he said with a mischievous grin, "get your costumes on!"

"Huh?" I said.

"I said go get dressed so you can get your treats. Didn't they teach you anything in school today?"

They did, but said nothing about begging door-to-door, which is how Nhanh subsequently explained it.

"Father won't like that," I said. "Begging isn't honorable. He'll just get mad."

We went inside and cousin Nhanh explained the deal to Father: how Halloween was America's Moon Festival where, in Vietnam, kids made lanterns and the best ones were awarded prizes as they walked around the neighborhood. "Same thing here," he concluded, "except the kids wear costumes and get candy. Play your cards right and we'll get some, too." Cousin Nhanh had all the makings of a heads-up American parent!

"Well," Father grunted, "as long as everyone else is doing it—and as long as everything is free."

It was already getting dark and since we had no budget for store-bought costumes, Cousin Nhanh got three paper grocery bags and cut eye holes in them, shoving them over our heads—even Tiny's, though the bag split going over his shoulders.

"There, now you all look like hideous brown ghosts. Take this pillow case and go get some candy. Just knock on each door, hold out the pillow case, and say, Trick-a-Cheat. That's all there is to it. You'll be eating candy for a month."

Unfortunately, even though it was supposed to be a big national holiday, very few residents of our Oakland neighborhood chose to answer their doorbells. This was partly because lots of people lived in big buildings where you needed a key to just get into the lobby and nobody felt like answering their buzzer just to run down stairs and give us something we didn't need. The other problem was that it was kind-of scary on Oakland streets after dark, with lots of big kids running around whooping and laughing and doing things that didn't seem to have much to do with honoring the dead. We finally fell-in with a platoon of little ghosts about our age who were making the rounds with their parents and we collected our fill with them. I had no idea who they were because everyone wore masks. Some of them could've been my schoolmates, but I didn't want to break-character and ask.

And cousin Nhanh was right. We had enough candy for a week, if not the month he promised. We even gave him a few pieces after our father ate his fill.

# 15

## I'll Wind

November brought cold wind and rain to Oakland. This was something we'd never experienced in An Hai, or even Hong Kong, although it was further north. Our clothes were designed for our bodies and our bodies were built for the tropics. We were sunfish in a freezer.

As California's winter storms hit one after another, we had no choice but to dress layer upon layer until we wore to school all the clothes we owned. Cousin Nhanh saw that part of our problem was cold feet, so he advised Father to replace our sandals with shoes, which he did. We didn't know we were supposed to wear socks with them, so our small toes immediately sprouted blisters. Cold water from puddles collected around our feet, so even indoors, our shivers got worse. It was only a matter of time until we all got sick, one after another like falling dominos. By the time Father took us to see a doctor using the first of our MediCal vouchers, our winter colds had become pneumonia.

We returned to the apartment loaded with pills. Since none of us could read English, the labels were useless so we took what seemed right in Father's best-guess, herbalist opinion. It didn't do much good. Our high fevers just made us feel colder, but Father persevered. He went to Merritt Lake and picked fresh eucalyptus and boiled the leaves in a pot, along with some lime and Chinese oil. He steamed our bodies under a blanket and in a few days, we got better. Since another major American holiday was approaching, Tiny declared it a Thanksgiving miracle. As he had spent as much time in church as at school, I figured he knew what he was talking about.

We got warm coats from a second-hand store and went back to school in a week. Despite Father's rule, Tiny now dawdled before coming home: listening to the sidewalk preachers and charity bell-ringers. Dimples asked how he could understand the preachers, since he had as little English as the rest of us, and he replied that language wasn't necessary to Hear the Word of God. When Father asked him why he always arrived home later than us girls, he gave one excuse after another: the teacher kept us late, or there was an assembly for older kids, or simply, upper grades are tougher and I need the extra help. Father didn't know enough about American education to question these explanations, so he didn't. Finally, Tiny had a better idea.

"I'll just invite some Bible people to our apartment," he said. "Father gets bored staying home all day. Some guests will cheer him up. He always says we should be hospitable to Americans."

Tiny hadn't lost his touch. A Salvation Army "captain" and a few of his helpers paid us a brief but courteous visit ending with a family prayer. I had no idea what they were saying, but my classroom acting allowed me to appear as interested and enthusiastic as Tiny, who actually managed to repeat some words. Whether or not his heavenly Jesus actually helped him to conquer English, his progress with our adopted language was extraordinary. He became a regular churchgoer, bringing back new Bible stories every Sunday. In a way, they were no more fantastic than the stories in Buddhist legends, and since America was a Christian country and our new home, learning them seemed to make more sense than tending our shrine. One Sunday morning, Dimples and I finally agreed to go with Tiny to one of the Baptist services and see what the shouting was all about. Maybe Jesus could help us with our English, too.

Unfortunately, Jesus saw through our ruse. English sounded as strange in church as it did on the street, so Tiny put the blame on us. "Just let the words wash over you," he said, "and let them take away your sins. People are people no matter where they live in the world. You don't have to speak to Jesus. The pastor does that for you. All you have to do is believe."

Tiny's conviction was impressive, but not persuasive. Learning anything is hard work—school was teaching us that—and while church might offer a divine shortcut to enlightenment, it was not the royal road to English. We girls wanted less work on weekends, not more, and Christian doctrine demanded extra effort. Although the old Tiny used to get mad when anyone crossed him, this new brother accepted us as "Doubting Thomases" and said he would pray for our understanding. That was fine with us—he could pray for us all day—but his devotion eventually got him into trouble.

It happened like this. Father respected Tiny's volunteer work for the church. He understood it would claim some after-school and weekend hours, but Father still insisted that Tiny do his household chores, excel at school, and observe our family rituals. On Grandpa's Death Commemoration Day—one of the many ancestral holidays when family members and close friends gather to show respect for departed elders—Tiny missed the traditional rites, this year held at our apartment. With at least thirty guests crowded into our living room—including Uncle Six and Cousin Nhanh with his five brothers—I watched the anger build on Father's face. Still, he kept things together until Tiny came through the door just as the guests were exchanging toasts.

Tiny cast a disapproving look at the multitude and spake, "The Lord condemns idol worshippers!"

Father choked on his beer, as did half the others. Dimples and I quietly backpedaled into the kitchen and listened for breaking furniture and breaking bones. Praise Jesus, it didn't happen.

"How dare you show your father such disrespect!" Uncle Six demanded.

"I am the Lord's son, and no one else's," Tiny said calmly.

"Ha!" Uncle Six cut his eyes to his younger brother and saw the powder keg was about to blow. The only way to stop a volcano is to give it another way to vent. "Ha Ha Ha!" he forced a laugh. One by one, the other guests laughed, too.

Finally Father hoisted his beer, "Then here's another toast—to all the fathers who watch over their families!"

"Hear, hear!" Uncle Six took a swig.

"Yes," Cousin Nhanh added, "This is a day for good thoughts and happy memories—a time for all men to be brothers!"

Others joined with similar toasts and the party got back on track. Tiny said nothing more. Without showing any emotion, he joined us girls in the kitchen and helped clean up after our guests.

We didn't know it at the time, but that Commemoration Day marked a turning point in the history of our family—and in our path to becoming Americans.

Father found that with a beer in his hand, he could better withstand both Tiny's Christian devil and the demons in his own soul. He was never without one again. The crowd in our living room that day never totally dispersed. Uncle Six, before this a rare visitor, became a fixture, joining us for nearly every meal. Cousin Nhanh, such a source of wisdom and common sense when we first arrived, visited rarely, and then mostly to check on us kids. Half the men from the party became Father's permanent crew. For the most part, they had been decent people in Vietnam—fathers, husbands, fishermen or farmers—but without their wives or families, they became unmoored and adrift on America's turbulent currents. Father drifted with them. When he spoke, it was in a drunken slur. When they talked about the past, it was with bitterness, not reverence or fond memories. When they talked of the future, it was about returning to drive the communists back to Hanoi. When they spoke of the present, it was to ask who was dealing the next hand of Tien Len or to demand more beer from us girls—their cocktail waitresses as soon as we returned from school—or argue about whose turn it was to go to the video store for the next dirty movie or to ante-up for this weekend's prostitute. We kids gave up our bedrooms to them. We slept and did homework in the living room then cleared out for school as soon as we heard Father stirring and put his breakfast on the table. Even worse, when his pals had drunk too much, they puked and wet their pants. We didn't touch the strangers, just endured their stink; but when Father soiled himself we felt obliged to clean him up, even if he passed out: ants rolling a heavy log. Tiny said there was a Hell. Dimples and I had found it.

After a month of this, Dimples and I went back to church with Tiny, if for no other reason than buy a few hours away from home.

"No evil will follow us here," Tiny said prophetically and we prayed that he was right. One sign this might be true was that there was a new minister at the church, Pastor Joseph, who spoke Vietnamese.

"Have faith in the Lord," Pastor Joseph said. Our native tongue sounded strange in an American church, smack in the middle of a big American city, but he made it sound comforting in a way Tiny never could. Pastor Joseph's Jesus sounded more like the Buddha: full of compassion and forgiveness rather than fire and brimstone. "The Lord is your only Father and Savior," he said gently.

"We already have a father," I said, mindful of Tiny's outburst on Commemoration Day.

"And God didn't save our family from falling apart," Dimples added.

The pastor was unfazed and invited us to join him on his knees, facing a beautifully carved crucifix. "Jesus, our Lord and Savior," he said solemnly, "show them the light. Make them realize the man they call father is an idol worshipper—"

"You worship an idol, too," Dimples interrupted him, pointing to the crucifix, "a dead man hanging on a cross."

Pastor Joseph chose to ignore her. He continued, "Give them the strength to turn away from the devil living within them. Amen."

We all stood together. Pastor Joseph faced Dimples directly. "Jesus Christ is not an idol. This is just his image, like a loved one's picture on your family altar. This is how the Faithful remember him, sacrificing himself for others and watching over us from heaven. The Bible is not a magic book. It is a testament of his teachings. Do you see the difference?"

Frankly, Dimples didn't and neither did I, and Tiny was far beyond questioning anything a man-of-the-cloth had to say; but there was a certain logic to his words and the peace they had brought into Tiny's troubled life was proof, at least for me, that Pastor Joseph and his church deserved respect.

Dimples and I left them praying and went home. We took the longest route we could.

# 16

## *Safe Harbor*

As if in answer to Pastor Joseph's prayer, Father and his gang were gone when we got home. In fact, they often went days between appearances: sometimes arriving late, after we'd gone to sleep, then leaving early; other times sleeping during the day when we were at school, then disappearing for the night. Consequently, we had the place mostly to ourselves but kept to our routines: Tiny cooking (when he wasn't working for the church), me cleaning and laundering, with Dimples helping out as best she could, which would've been more if she had been taller, like tending the family altar which now sort-of freaked me out after Pastor Joseph's sermon.

When winter storms didn't rake us, the city was cold and clear. The apartment never seemed warm enough and because there was no heater, we walked around wearing blankets and bedspreads, like American Indians. Still, between school and an intermittently peaceful life, our apartment became an island of repose, if a lonely one. Despite his faults, we still loved Father. We talked occasionally about his better days in the village and appreciated all he had tried to do for us in the camp. As for Mama and Pudgy and Brat and Fly Swat, I would've given all that I owned, or ever would own, just to see them one more time. Dimples was getting along fine now, in school and out, so I dared not voice these thoughts, which would surely start her crying or make her act out—but that never stopped me from thinking them.

Then late one afternoon, when things were blessedly quiet and we were fixing dinner, we heard a knock on the door. It couldn't be Father because he had a key, and it couldn't be some of his gang because they didn't come here without Father. Maybe it was cousin Nhanh on one of his rare visits. We all ran to the door to greet him.

Instead of Nhanh, it was a well-fed, middle-aged Asian woman in western dress who looked so normal we almost cried. She said something in English that even Tiny didn't understand, then pointed to herself and repeated it. More blank stares. Then she repeated herself in Cantonese. I had picked up some of that language in Hong Kong, so I made out more of what she said, though she was a pretty fast talker. "May," she said, "my name is May. I'm your landlady. I live downstairs with my two-year old daughter, Tanya. I've kept my eye on your apartment. You used to have lots of people around, but now, not so much. I just see you kids coming and going to school, bringing food back from the cafeteria. I just want you to know that if you're having trouble, I'm willing to help. Come downstairs—I'll show you my place."

This was actually the first building resident we'd met, so going into another unit, especially the owner's, felt strange. Her apartment was decked-out like old Shanghai, with lots of family heirlooms and a well-kept family shrine. It almost felt like home. The only thing odd about it was Tanya, who looked more like one of the black toddlers we saw in strollers at the supermarket.

"My husband is African-American," she explained. "Look—here's his picture." The framed wall photo showed a handsome black man in a sharp business suit. He was big as a house, as many black men seemed to be, but unlike Mr. Richmond, looked very athletic. His hair, though, was a big black puffball. We'd seen those in our neighborhood, but usually on teens with their bell-bottom trousers, tight shirts, or black girls with clogged shoes and long, colored fingernails. May, also dressed-up for this photograph, looked like a school girl by comparison. But she obvious loved and respected her husband. "He's a very successful businessman," she beamed. He had a lot of hats scattered around the house—baseball caps, wide-brimmed straw hats, as well as a fedora or two, but I had no idea how he could wear them over that Afro. Tanya was a plump, good-natured little kid with a runny nose who said little more than, "Who dis? Who dat?" while she pointed to us. She reminded me of Pudgy and Fly Swat wrapped up in one package. I had nothing to say that she could understand, so I just tickled her under her chin and made her giggle.

Now that we had a friend in the building, I spent a lot of time at May's. The biggest gift she gave me was to increase my English skills even as I improved my Cantonese. With her help, my grades in school shot up and I no longer had to act like a good student—I was one. She even had a car and drove us all over town like a personal chauffer. Whenever she had something extra, like storage jars or cosmetic samples from a department store, she gave them to us. Dimples and I began going to school with rosy cheeks, red nails and perfume that made us smell like money. Our teachers explained that was not "age appropriate," so that phase of becoming Americans had to wait a while longer. But May had a big influence on our young lives—all of it good.

Even when Father was home, May checked on us—especially when Father was home. Thankfully, he did not view this as an intrusion. He was still in awe of authority figures and always anxious to impress them, so whenever our landlady knocked on the door and announced herself, he straightened things up and put his open beer in the 'fridge and made himself presentable. She asked how we were doing and often brought us little gifts. She even helped Father understand some of the government forms and notices we got in the mail—important to getting her rent, of course, but it saved us a trip to consult cousin Nhanh who was seldom at home. Father even encouraged us to drop by May's apartment and ask what we could do to help, like babysit Tanya if she had to go out. "It's only common courtesy," he said, but I was happy to do it.

The only one who wasn't happy with the arrangement was Dimples. She vividly remembered Father's girlfriend in Hong Kong and the incident with Uncle Six and the traffic. Her old fear and resentment of Father began to resurface, fueled by her distrust of our new friend. She was afraid Father was falling in love with May, and that meant nothing but trouble.

"How can they even like each other?" Dimples asked one evening, doing an exceptionally poor job of washing plates after dinner. "The only English Father knows is hi, bye, and thank you. He can't even speak Cantonese. And she's married to a rich man. Father doesn't have a nickel!"

Somehow, Father had money for beer, but that wasn't the point. May loved her husband and had her own family and as far as I could tell, she was just a good person who liked helping others—but Dimples would have none of that. Her mind was made up.

"Well," I replied, "we can't control what Father does, but May has done plenty for us. I get A's on my homework now and can talk to my teacher and the kids at school. You do what you want, but I'm still going to be her friend."

Things got resolved on our second American holiday, a food-day called Thanksgiving. As near as I could figure, it commemorated a time when the pioneers and Indians stopped fighting long enough to share a nice dinner, then went back to killing each other. Since almost all Buddhist holidays involve some kind of food and dead people, this holiday made perfect sense. As it turned out, we had three Thanksgiving meals that day when one would have been plenty.

The first meal was our school lunch. The cafeteria served a tough, stringy bird called a turkey which tasted like my blanket. At least I understood now why we had spent hours earlier that week making paper turkeys: the old bird tasted like cardboard. Our second meal was at May's, which all of us attended, even Dimples—though she just glared at her plate and didn't say a word. The bird was just as bad but because I could make small-talk, we had a nice visit before graciously thanking our host and getting Father back to his beer.

The last meal was at Tiny's church, a buffet following the evening service. Enough with all the turkey! At least I knew why the pioneers and Indians went back to war as soon as they cleared the table—each side refused to eat the last piece! Anyway, Dimples and I attended, partly to leave Father alone with his beer and partly because the church was one of the few places we felt safe and comforted even when other parts of our life weren't so hot. It was even worth staring down at one more slice of dead bird. Personally, I liked seeing happy families together—parents and their children of all ages, some with grandparents and aunts and uncles—as it had been a long time since we'd enjoyed that. It made me homesick, but in good way.

Dimples and I sat to one side, pretending to enjoy our turkey while taking in the show. "Now," I said softly, "aren't you glad you came?"

Dimples looked around. Everyone in Tiny's church was American. Not that all were white—some were black and some were Mexican and a few were Asian like us—but they all ate their leathery turkey with knives and forks and didn't use chopsticks and nobody was drunk and everyone had a smile on their face.

When we finished, we put our paper plates and plastic utensils in the trash and Dimples said, "I guess we should pray."

We went to the spot where we had first met Pastor Joseph and got down on our knees, folded our hands in front of our chest and bowed our heads.

"Speak American," Dimples whispered then looked up at the crucifix. "Look at the statue. He's American."

I looked up, eyes watering. I wasn't sure she was right, but she sounded certain. We both lowered our heads again and closed our eyes. I spoke softly in English.

"Bless this house, O Lord, we pray. Make it safe by night and day. My family together." I nudged Dimples with my elbow and whispered, "Say amen."

"Amen," Dimples said in flawless American.

The year ended with our new country's two favorite holidays: Christmas and New Year's. I knew the first had something to do with Jesus and a fat bearded man but I completely misunderstood the second. The coming month would clarify both.

On December 1, 1979, we received our government food grant for the month. Father dispatched Dimples and me to Lucky with instructions to stretch it as far as it would go before digging into our extra cash.

Greeting us outside the Lucky store was a fat man in a red suit, red hat, and phony white beard. He was ringing a bell beside a steel pot into which passers-by occasionally dropped coins, so I figured this strange creature represented the poor odd-balls who were America's object of charity. If not, the fat man made a pretty good living for a ringing a bell that was more annoying than musical. We gave him a wide berth and side-stepped through the sliding door only to be hit with a hundred other images of this same guy stuck on banners and packages and labels, often surrounded by leaves, red berries, horned animals, and midgets. Huh?

I found out about "Sandy Claws" the next day at school. Contrary to my guess, he was not the symbolic receiver of gifts, he was the giver. His job was to fly around the world in a wheeless cart pulled by eight tiny deer (okay—we had those in Vietnam, but only in the highlands and their horns were way smaller than these big antlers) and leave presents at every single, solitary house by sliding down into the fireplace. This seemed like an impossible job. I knew how long it took just to fly from Hong Kong to San Francisco and that took more than one night! But it was made easier, and made more sense, when Miss Lincoln said that only "good boys and girls" got gifts, which if the kids in my own village and in the camps were any guide, would shorten his route considerably. She didn't say why the stores displayed special signs and everybody lined up to spend extra money on extra things they didn't need, but I assumed she would cover that tomorrow.

That evening at home, Dimples asked, "Am I a good girl?"

I thought about that long enough to make her suspicious then said, "Sure."

"Then why didn't I get any gifts last Christmas?"

Another pause. "Because we were in An Hai. They don't have Christmas in Vietnam, remember? It's an American holiday."

That brought us back to Santa's world-wide mission, which still didn't make sense unless he was magic and the reindeer were dragons or something like that, so we let it slide. The gift idea was appealing, though, so we decided to behave ourselves for the rest of the month, just to see what happened.

"Okay," Dimples said later as I was trying to do some homework. "How is Sandy Claws going to get into our apartment? We don't have a fireplace." She was obviously overthinking the problem.

"Well, maybe he knocks on the door. I don't know. We'll find out. I gotta get this done."

Still, this was a nagging question, as was the reason people put dead pine trees in their living room and spent even more time and money hanging stuff on them to make them not look like pine trees. Miss Lincoln never got into this, she said, because it was based on a particular religion and she wasn't supposed to talk about that in school, so the natural person to ask was Tiny. He knew all about such things.

"The pine tree is an evergreen—a symbol of eternal life," he said, "like the everlasting life Jesus offers us in heaven."

Here we go again with Jesus, but at least this explanation made sense. I asked him if the lists the other kids made and sent in letters to the North Pole were really prayers to Sandy Claws asking for specific gifts. He said yes, but the whole idea of gift-giving came from the Three Wise Men who visited Jesus on his birthday which was the reason for the holiday, yada, yada, yada. As I tuned-out the sermon, I looked at Dimples and saw we had the same idea. Maybe we could write a letter to Sandy Claws asking him to deliver Mama and our sister and brothers to us for Christmas. After all, we now lived in America and, according to the rules, he is supposed to visit every house and we had already sworn to be good all month. But if that was possible, why hadn't cousin Nhanh just asked Sandy Claws to bring us straight to Oakland, saving us the perils at sea and harrowing stay in the refugee camps? It didn't make sense, which started me thinking that maybe the whole holiday was made-up, which meant Tiny's story about evergreens and the Wise Men was made up too, which cast Jesus and The Bible in doubt, which would also explain why the dead ancestors and mythical beings, like the Buddha and Quang Am and Father Dragon we prayed to year-after-year in Vietnam never seemed to answer our prayers. My head began to hurt. None of this had anything to do with my schoolwork, which (aside from Father's drinking and May's kindness and our government assistance) were the only things that really affected our lives.

To heck with Christmas, I finally told myself, which really killed my holiday spirit. Dimples had come to the same conclusion and overnight, our house ran out of laughter. When Cleveland Elementary School recessed for the holidays, we lost our last link to the sunny side of life. Everything was gray, cloudy, and cold: inside our apartment and out.

Change came, but from an unlikely place. When Father was sober, he was the father we remembered: strong, demanding, gruff—but loving in his way, the way a captain pushes his crew to keep everyone safe. When he was drunk, this façade fell away and he sometimes wept openly for his wife and the children he left behind. We got used to both of these fathers, sometimes inhabiting the same house on the same day, but one time, near Christmas Day, when Father was sitting with his beer and blanket on the couch, he noticed Dimples and I had been crying—feeling especially sorry for ourselves—and motioned for us to come over, which we did. He opened his blanket to admit Dimples, who snuggled close against him, her sobs reduced to a whimper, then he looked at me.

"What are you crying about?" he asked in a stern voice, the way he sounded when he was sober.

"I—I miss Mama," I said, tears starting again, "I wish—"

The flat of his hand caught my cheek. "I wish you would shut up!" he said firmly. "You walk around here like your little sister, simpering like a baby or with your head up in the clouds! What good does that do you? What does it do for anybody? Nothing! Grow up! You're not a little kid any more. You're a young woman. Act like one! What do you think your mother would do?"

I don't know if the slap or the question startled me more, but his last question woke me up. What would Mama do in this situation? What would she have done throughout the whole year-long voyage that brought me to this moment? There's no way I could know, but one thing was certain: Father was right. She would not walk around crying like a baby. She would take care of her family and herself.

About then, Tiny came home and I slithered into the kitchen, trying to decide what I should do next. Since the debacle on Commemoration Day, Father and Tiny had avoided each other like the plague, barely saying two words to each other unless it was strictly necessary. Now I was happy to have another castaway at my side. Now I finally knew what my big brother was going through. Our childhood roots run deep, especially through the rough soil of bad memories, but you either take what nourishment you can and rise to blossom or you let hard knocks stunt your growth. The choice wasn't up to the Buddha or Jesus or Father Dragon or even Father, it was up to me. Like Tiny, I had decided to grow up.

Christmas came and went. Sandy Claws didn't. If he passed our small apartment, it was while I was asleep and dreaming of Mama. In my dream, she did what good mothers always do: comforted me with words and gestures, told me to be brave and strong and true. Stroking my hair, she reminded me that she, too, was forced to become a woman overnight: engaged and married at a too-young age.

"I don't want to be you," I told her in my dream.

"Then be yourself," she answered. "You have two arms and two legs. You have good health and your friends and family. Some women have none of that, so you're starting out ahead of the game. Your life is in America now. Live in the past and you will lose your future. You can't eat the same meal twice, so move on. Embrace the world. There's more to it than you can imagine!"

School was still on break, so Dimples and I made our own Christmas using the remains of everyone else's. People tossed away all kinds of things after the holiday and trash cans and dumpsters became our department store. We culled empty boxes, crumpled wrapping paper, pretty ribbons almost intact, tons and tons of flowery bows. We took the choice bits home then went to opposite ends of the living room to make each other secret gifts. Before long, Dimples appeared with a gift box wrapped with strips of paper clipped from bigger pieces. It was wrapped with a ribbon that looked new and three or four bows of different colors. "Open it!" she said, but I was reluctant to destroy a masterpiece. "Come on," she thrust it at me again, "Open it!" I suppose creation and destruction are just part of life's cycle, so I did what I thought would please her and wrecked her hard work. She loved it.

Inside the box was a heart-shaped pouch made from smaller pieces of cardboard but decorated like the package itself, covered with bits of uncooked rice glued-on like glitter. This girl had not been wasting her time in kindergarten! Inside the heart-pouch was another paper heart, then another, then another, each one smaller until they totaled twelve—the number of animals in the Chinese zodiac. She then took two of the smallest ones, put a dab of rubber cement on each, and pressed them onto my ear lobes.

"There," she said proudly, "I also gave you new ear rings for Christmas!"

"I feel like a princess," I said, though I really felt like a mother very proud of her little girl.

"Sit up straight," Dimples said, studying the fit of her creation. "There. Show them off properly!"

Now who's the mother?

"Okay," she continued, completely absorbed in my makeover, "now you need a necklace to go with them." She took a longer piece of ribbon, glued the remaining flat hearts to it in an order that made sense to her then held it up to my neck. The ribbon was too short to tie, so she glued the necklace on me, too. Of course, rubber cement sticks to your skin just fine until you want the glue to last, so my inventive gifts fell off almost as soon as Dimples finished. I saw she was getting frustrated—with the glue, with the bogus Sandy Claws who skipped our house, with me, with herself—so I took her hands and said, "Look, that was fun but it's enough Christmas for one day. Let's have Christmas again tomorrow. And the day after that! We still have plenty of paper and cardboard and ribbons, and if we run out we'll get more until the trash collectors dump the garbage. What do you think?"

She thought that was a cool idea, so that's what we did; only the next day, we worried less about duplicating an American Christmas and more about just making the things we liked—toys and figures we'd learned to make back home: small paper kites, folded birds and fish, tiny circles and stars. We might be stuck in Oakland—with its well-fed athletic people who used cars instead of feet, had sharp eyes they hid behind sun glasses, talked on phones when they could chat on sidewalks—but An Hai, mother to us both, would always be safe in our hearts.

New Year's Eve was the last holiday on America's calendar. Although Vietnamese Tet occurred a month later, it was for both peoples the end of one thing and the beginning of something else. While the West measured time by the masculine sun and the East by the feminine Moon, the two ways of life occasionally joined, just as men and women make their way in the world: sometimes alone and sometimes together, but in the long run as a family. That's how we three kids felt as we leaned from our window on that chilly December midnight watching cars honk and people laugh and cavort in the street. They hugged and kissed and raised the dead with noisemakers. Fireworks went off. Suddenly, spontaneously, they all began counting at once:

Ten, nine, eight...

The New Year was fast approaching. I was promoted from eight to nine.

Seven, six, five...

Dimples, too, would move on to seven—though it felt like we'd both put ten years under our belts since that first awful night on the boat.

Four, three, two...

Four—the number of our family members in Oakland and the number of family members waiting to join us from An Hai.

One...Happy New Year!

The crowd erupted below us: screeching, singing, and clapping. I felt like they were cheering for me.

# 17

## *Smooth Sailing*

In 1983, Mama, Pudgy, Brat, and Fly Swat came to the United States. They passed through the same crucible of water and fire as we did: floating refugees at sea, then as inmates in the tsunami of fugitives that had gradually ebbed to a flood. They found solace with the Catholics in Hong Kong and used that strength to survive the camps. They, too, rode the soaring seabird to America, sponsored by the Baptist Church. It seems there was room in Jesus's heart for more of us than Tiny.

In 1984, Mama and Father added a new baby to our household: a genuine, made-in-America, birth-certified U.S. citizen that brought our family head-count to nine. Apparently our parents used the first year of their American reunion wisely. I have no idea what they said to each other in the deep hours of the night as they became re-acquainted, but what could not be forgotten was forgiven. Our family was finally together and stayed that way.

Not that some things didn't change. When Mama and the others got off the plane in San Francisco, I was Americanized enough to give them a big hug—a public display of affection. This seemed to make Mama uncomfortable, but like most mothers she quickly came to like it. We never became what Americans would call a "huggy" family, but we got used to letting our emotions speak-up when they had to and not keep even our positive feelings forever bottled up.

But more than a few things stayed the same. The supernatural forces that shaped, and continued to shape, life in Vietnamese culture had not disappeared. In fact, America's energy only added to their power. Nothing is lost in the universe; it can only be transformed. I look at my life, from start to its eventual finish, as a huge wheel that turns forever. When we act in harmony with its rhythms, when we dance to the music of life, we draw strength and happiness that can make others stronger and happier, too. Mama always told us to never take more than we need and to share with others what we can spare. That continues to be good advice.

In the summer of 1992, I returned to Vietnam, to Da Nang and An Hai on the banks of the Song Hang River. Like any adult returning to a childhood home, I found the scene surreal: partly what I remembered, partly what I only imaged, partly completely different—the substance of a new generation. Nobody knew (or if they did, they didn't say) where my stay-behind relatives lived—I only ran into a few by accident when I stumbled onto my old house. They invited me inside where years and pretense fell away. We gossiped. I answered questions about America and those in our family who had gone there. I became a village curiosity. My old house filled with visitors of every age and I talked and laughed till I was hoarse. Then, when shadows lengthened and it was time to go, my hosts took me to the family Worship Room, now a shrine for thirty people and I lit incense and prayed with my extended family. What I accepted without question as a Vietnamese kid, then rejected in America, I now embraced as a citizen of the universe. I felt that universe smile back at me with its usual, kindly indifference.

Was all our pain and suffering worth it? Is the pain and suffering of childbirth worth a baby? You decide. Would I repeat my long voyage to America and womanhood even if success was not assured? You bet. Water leaves its source not knowing which obstacles it will encounter. All it can do is behave according to its nature: finding a path here, making a path there, pooling its strength when needed until it can break free. Ultimately, it reaches the sea, the mother of us all. That sea gave birth to the person I became in America. I am thankful to be its daughter.

*In Loving Memory of Jiep Thi Le*

*February 18th, 1971 – December 19th, 2017*

# Editors Notes

www.ingramcontent.com/pod-product-compliance
Lightning Source LLC
Chambersburg PA
CBHW070918080526
44589CB00013B/1354